Hoosier Latinos

Latin America

MEXICO

THE BAHAMAS

CUBA

CAYMAN ISLANDS

HAITI

JAMAICA

DOMINICAN REPUBLIC

PUERTO RICO

MARTINIQUE
ST. LUCIA

BELIZE

HONDURAS

GUATEMALA
EL SALVADOR

NICARAGUA

PANAMA

COSTA RICA

ST. VINCENT AND THE GRENADINES

GRENADA

TRINIDAD AND TOBAGO

VENEZUELA

GUYANA

SURINAME

FRENCH GUIANA

COLOMBIA

ECUADOR

PERU

BRAZIL

BOLIVIA

South Pacific Ocean

PARAGUAY

CHILE

ARGENTINA

URUGUAY

South Atlantic Ocean

FALKLAND ISLANDS

Map by Bruce Jones, brucejonesdesign.com

Hoosier Latinos

A Century of Struggle, Service, and Success

Nicole Martinez–LeGrand *and* Daniel Gonzales
With Foreword by Sujey Vega

Indiana Historical Society Press | Indianapolis | 2022

Printed in the United States of America

This book is a publication of the
Indiana Historical Society Press
Eugene and Marilyn Glick Indiana History Center
450 West Ohio Street
Indianapolis, Indiana 46202-3269 USA
www.indianahistory.org
Telephone orders: 1-317-234-0020
Online orders: http://shop.indianahistory.org

The paper in this publication meets the minimum requirements of American National Standard for Information Sciences—Permanence of Paper for Printed Library Materials, ANSI Z39. 48–1984

Library of Congress Cataloging-in-Publication Data

Names: Martinez-LeGrand, Nicole, author. | Gonzales, Daniel, author. |
  Vega, Sujey, writer of foreword.
Title: Hoosier Latinos : a century of struggle, service, and success /
  Nicole Martinez-LeGrand and Daniel Gonzales ; with foreword by Sujey
  Vega.
Description: Indianapolis : Indiana Historical Society Press, 2022. |
  Includes bibliographical references and index.
Identifiers: LCCN 2021058569 (print) | LCCN 2021058570 (ebook) | ISBN
  9780871954626 (paperback) | ISBN 9780871954633 (epub)
Subjects: LCSH: Hispanic Americans--Indiana--History. | Hispanic
  Americans—Indiana—Social conditions. | Hispanic
  Americans—Indiana—Ethnic identity. | Indiana—Ethnic relations. |
  Indiana—Social conditions.
Classification: LCC F535.S75 M37 2022 (print) | LCC F535.S75 (ebook) |
  DDC 977.2/00468—dc23/eng/20211222
LC record available at https://lccn.loc.gov/2021058569
LC ebook record available at https://lccn.loc.gov/2021058570

To Madeleine, William, and Charlie

Remember that in this world, you are what you leave behind. These stories and this history—your history—is a gift to you.

Made possible by a generous grant from
Lilly Endowment, Inc.

Contents

Consuelo "Connie" Figueroa (woman on right) with friends, celebrating *Fiestas Patrias* (Mexican Independence Day) in East Chicago, ca. 1940s

Foreword

Recalling, Reclaiming, and Remembering Latino Hoosiers at the Crossroads of America

It is hard to imagine twenty years have passed since I first drove through the Midwest in search of higher education. I was a wide-eyed student when I first set sights on the cornfields and small towns of Iowa, Kansas, Illinois, and Indiana. Intimidated and excited to go out on my own for graduate school, I reminded myself of the struggles my parents went through when leaving their families behind in Mexico. I looked upon the University of Illinois's campus quad in Urbana–Champaign and shed a tear, knowing that the buildings of academia were precisely what my parents had sacrificed for. Still, without family nearby, the Midwest felt completely foreign to this California/Texas Chicana. I felt lost, misplaced, and alien in this heartland of the United States. After several weeks of feeling lonely, craving the tastes of home, and missing the sounds of Spanish, my partner (now husband) moved to Lafayette, Indiana, and changed the trajectory of my life.

While in graduate school, we took turns visiting each other over the weekends. He would drive to Champaign, and I would meet him in Lafayette. For me, the entrance ramp onto I-74 eastbound was cathartic. I could literally leave the pain and stress of UIUC behind me and happily head to the "Crossroads of America."[1] Once in Lafayette, I would drive down Columbia Street and every now and then hear the familiar sounds of *norteño* music bumping out of someone's car. I could count on packed Spanish services on Sundays at Saint Boniface and warm *empanadas* (filled pastries, fried or baked) from Mamá Inés Mexican Bakery (*panaderia*). If I needed ingredients to approximate my mother's cooking, I had multiple Latino-owned grocery stories to choose from. I relished my weekends in greater Lafayette and despised returning to Illinois. There was

something so welcoming, cozy, and familiar about maneuvering through Lafayette. I did not have to try as hard to justify my being there as I did with Champaign. I could find community in Indiana. I could feel less foreign in a town where I was not such an anomaly.

I later set out to study this feeling, interview the families that made Lafayette home, and search for the way Latino belonging uniquely operated in this small Indiana city. My 2015 book, *Latino Heartland: Of Borders and Belonging in the Midwest* (2015), came out of this quest. I wanted to understand how a thriving Spanish-speaking community came to claim central Indiana as home.[2] Similarly, the Latino History Project at the Indiana Historical Society set out to document the incredibly rich history of Latinos/as throughout the state of Indiana. Using oral history and archival records, *Hoosier Latinos: A Century of Struggle, Service, and Success* recognizes the impressive lineage of Latinos/as in Indiana across time and space. Inclusive of both traditional and nontraditional settling destinations throughout Indiana, *Hoosier Latinos* takes the reader from Northwest Indiana to Indianapolis and even as far south as Evansville to explore how Latino Hoosiers navigated home and belonging in this midwestern state. Importantly, the authors include impressive archival research to locate the Latino presence in Indiana as far back as the 1800s. Though my own work includes historical comparative experiences with Native Americans, Black freedmen, and German immigrants in Lafayette, the Latino history in *Latino Heartland* (2015) only goes back to the 1950s. In contrast, Nicole Martinez–LeGrand and Daniel Gonzales present a profound history of Latino Hoosiers through an intensive exploration of records and delightful conversations with those still living who were able to share the history of Indiana's Latino past.

Weaving archival findings together with oral history narratives, *Hoosier Latinos* brings to light the beauty and adversity of Latinos in Indiana. Martinez–LeGrand and Gonzales center the voices of these instrumental Hoosier families to finally give them a place at the proverbial crossroads. This book is important because it provides an invaluable look at the lives of Latinos throughout Indiana history, placing them at the center and recognizing their contributions across the state. This is an admirable project, and one that the authors take on with great success. *Hoosier Latinos* validates the experience of so many Latinos who made Indiana home for more than a century. It also provides non-Latino Hoosiers a chance to identify and understand how their Latino neighbors became valid, equal partners in the making of Hoosier–Latino identity. As such, the book proves to be an excellent resource for educators and individuals alike who are open to exploring the role of Latinos in their own towns.

At the close of my book, I suggest that "we must go about the difficult task of creating a collective community that embraces its complexity." I see *Hoosier Latinos* taking on that recommendation by providing an excellent voyage across the complexity of Indiana's construction. As a researcher, I can vividly remember how excited I would get when I briefly saw Indiana tangentially mentioned in Latino history books (Terre Haute has a brief mention in the famous *Decade of Betrayal*, a book often cited in Chicano history). What I would have given to have had a book like

Hoosier Latinos decades ago.[3] Additionally, *Hoosier Latinos* encourages communities to document their own pasts and collect oral histories. Access to the Indiana Historical Society's detailed oral histories and vivid images in its online repository provides researchers with excellent primary materials to explore the history of Indiana. It is a treasure for students, educators, and Hoosier residents.

I personally connected with the narratives that illustrated the growth of Latinos in Northwest Indiana. While my own scholarship highlights the greater Lafayette area, I unknowingly had family history in both Gary and Hammond, Indiana. My mother's side of my family tree has several branches in Indiana. In Hammond I have my mother's cousin, Sergio Ferrer Ceja and his family. Moving up the tree one generation, my mother's godparents, Sara Prado and Luis Espinoza, lived in Gary until Luis retired and moved to Zamora, Michoacán, Mexico. They never had children of their own, but my mother received gifts from money earned in Indiana. In fact, when I returned to Michoacán for my maternal grandmother's funeral, I found among her things a metal union card for a Louis Espinoza. Issued by the United Steelworkers Local 1010 in Hammond, it is signed by president I. W. Abel. I am therefore able to date this union card somewhere between 1965 and 1977, which were the dates of Abel's union presidency.[4]

Climbing further up my family tree, my *abuelita* (grandmother) related a story about her father, my great-grandfather José Espinoza, and his exploits in the Midwest. It seems José, like many men of his generation, traveled for seasonal work to the United States. When my grandmother was an infant, he brought her back a pair of gold earrings. Known as *arracadas*, or small hoops, I still have these earrings as a memory of her

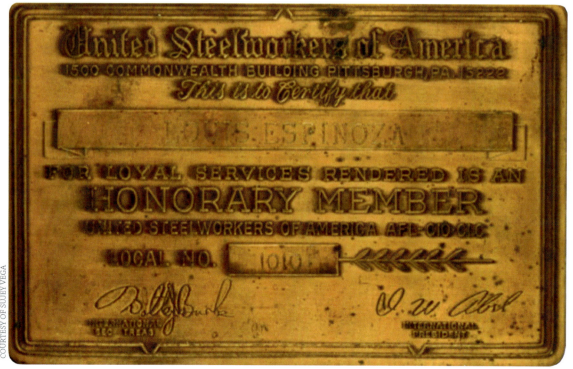

Steelworker's union card for Luis Espinoza, Hammond, Indiana, ca. 1965–77

and of her father's journey to El Norte (the North; that is, the United States).

My *abuelita* told me about a time when José was working somewhere in Michigan and got himself arrested after getting into a fistfight with another man. Once released, the brother of the other assailant warned José that it might be best if he skipped town. Fearing for his life, my great-grandfather fled to the only place where he had friends and family—Gary, Indiana. There he found refuge and earned enough money to get himself safely back to my grandmother in Mexico. Though much is missing from the story, my grandmother remembered very well the importance that Indiana held in saving her father's life.

Hoosier Latinos provides an exciting opportunity to understand what my great-grandfather José and his kinfolk Luis experienced while in Gary and Hammond. Like me, my great-grandfather found refuge in Indiana. Though I never met him, reading the stories of other Latinos in Northwest Indiana helped me feel closer to him, especially after learning about Gary's Latino community that had welcomed him in his time of need.

While *Hoosier Latinos* connects me to my own lineage in Indiana's past, it also provides deeper scholarly perspectives that will be useful to educators and researchers alike. What follows are five specific contributions or useful themes in this work. While reading *Hoosier Latinos* helped me reach into the lives of my *antepasados* (ancestors), I hope it can entice readers to continue exploring how their own history plays out in this volume.

Contribution 1: Latino Palimpsests in Indiana

What is a palimpsest and why is it relevant to Latino Hoosiers? A palimpsest has to do with layering and the stratification of time. For instance, when remodeling a bathroom in an older home, there is the tedious process of peeling away outdated wallpaper. Once started, one begins to see a paper mosaic of history. Decades of décor trends appear in these layers of the past. Shiplap (boards, side by side) gives way to metallic art deco designs and somewhere on top are torn pieces of bright yellow daisies. Traces of previous residents peak through to the present. This interwoven view of various wallpapers is a palimpsest.

Mamá Inés's Bakery in Lafayette, Indiana

Similarly, Indiana is layered with palimpsests of various peoples. Native American street names lead up to German houses of worship, which are catty-cornered with once-abandoned strip malls revitalized by Spanish-speaking entrepreneurs. These palimpsests of people beckon us to pay attention and appreciate how their overlapping lives built the very spaces we inhabit today.

Hoosier Latinos recognizes these layered pasts by emphasizing "the importance of weaving Latino history into the state's broader historical narrative." Dating as far back as the 1800s, Latino residents of Indiana commingled with the German families, Irish workers, and freed Blacks that made this state home. These communities navigated the land once inhabited by Shawnee, Miami, Lenape, and Potawatomi peoples. The palimpsests of Indiana's past were not always harmonious, and in some cases were quite violent. Think of Indian removals, lynchings, and the reign of the Ku Klux Klan. Still, these layers define where the state has come from and how it continues to evolve. Martinez–LeGrand and Gonzales seek to recognize another layer to this past, one that spans generations and reaches to multiple regions of Indiana. Incorporating the role Latinos played in the state's history shows a dedication to honoring the past by exploring its complicated reality.

They further describe how migrant labor housing was converted from a stagecoach stop, illustrating a palimpsest of various moments in Indiana's history. Through their exploration of records, the reader can imagine horse-drawn carriages rolling past a Mexican photographer's studio in Indianapolis in 1878. One could relive the Depression era anxieties of deported families who were forced to board trains to Mexico. Years later, many came back and were recruited to fill the industrial and agricultural labor shortages during World War II.

While *Hoosier Latinos* recognizes the historical and numerical importance of Latinos in Northwest Indiana and in Indianapolis, the authors note the impact of residents in smaller communities, as well. For instance, some of the migrant laborers chose to settle in smaller towns throughout the state. Although cities such as Indianapolis and the Indiana Harbor region attracted thriving communities of Latinos, other scholarship reminds us to look at Latinos in smaller towns for their Hoosier experiences. Martinez–LeGrand's interview with 97-year-old Raúl Piñon, his wife Rogelia (83), and their children Horace and Hope, illustrates the arrival and survival of a family at Mount Summit, Indiana. While the total population growth in places like Indianapolis was much higher, the percentage growth in these smaller towns was certainly significant, as well. Recent growth and demographic changes in towns such as Lafayette, Frankfort, Goshen, and Evansville, Indiana, prove the need for further research in these types of places. *Hoosier Latinos* will inspire others to do their own exploration and conduct oral histories in order to recognize how Latino families contributed to both the large cities and small towns of Indiana.

Contribution 2: Indiana's *Paisa* Network

As Latinos arrived and settled across Indiana, they relied on what I term the "*paisa* network." *Paisa* is a Spanish word that roughly translates to someone who hails from your hometown. For Latinos, and Mexicans in the United States specifically, *paisa* came to mean anyone from their home country. I remember conducting interviews in Lafayette with librarian Monica Casanova who notably explained the importance of "helping out our *paisas*." Although Monica's family had settled in Indiana in the early 1990s, she still felt called to offer aid to newly arriving Latinos. This commitment to help out fellow countrymen and women resonates in the interviews collected in *Hoosier Latinos*. In her interview, Irene Osario explained that Latino entrepreneurs "did a lot of bartering with the other little businesses in the neighborhood." She went on to recall how her family's printing press supplied wrapping paper to others in exchange for cheese and chocolates in order "to help each other out" during the 1920s.

The *paisa* network also helps us recognize the significant contributions of Carmen Velásquez during the Civil Rights era in Indiana. *Hoosier Latinos* highlights the migrant organizing efforts of Velásquez and rightly situates her in the pantheon of Chicano/a activists such as César Chávez and Dolores Huerta. As a leader in the Associated Migrant Opportunities Services (AMOS) in the 1970s, Velásquez traversed Grant County, Indiana, to improve the quality of life for *paisas* in migrant labor camps. The commitment Velásquez and other AMOS staff showed to the thousands of migrant farmworkers in "forty-two migrant camps across Indiana" demonstrates the crucial role of the *paisa* network in Latino lives. Her leadership and tireless efforts earned Carmen Velásquez a prime place in Indiana's history. As a woman, as a Chicana, and as a Hoosier, Velásquez modeled how to make transformative change in otherwise daunting circumstances.

The *paisa* network is evident in AMOS's herculean efforts across Indiana, but the network also functioned in small-scale personal interactions. *Hoosier Latinos* provides ample vignettes of how Latino and Hispanic communities helped out their arriving countrymen, regardless if they knew one another or not. Chapter three relates how seasonal farmworkers, Raúl and Rogelia Piñon, left Texas to settle in Mount Summit, Indiana. With the migrant campus closed for winter, the family struggled to find housing. Noticing the family's needs, José Morales stepped in and provided assistance for these strangers. Whether it was the Block and Pennsy neighborhood of Indiana Harbor or the cold wintry streets of Mount Summit, we see how early Latino social networks built community. And as I noted in *Latino Heartland* (2015), this *paisa* network remains to this day. Latinos continue to aid each other in making homes and utilizing their networks to navigate the midwestern landscape.

Contribution 3: Latino Investments in Indiana

Significantly, economic contributions from Latinos have been around for a while and have resulted in financial reciprocity. Indiana has provided Latino families with steady employment. In turn, these families have set up businesses, purchased homes, paid taxes, and spent their money in the local economy. Thus, not only have migrant laborers helped harvest the food placed on America's dining room table, but also Latino entrepreneurs and blue-collar workers have directly strengthened Indiana's GDP.

Actively recruited and then summarily forsaken during times of American economic decline, the stories of Latinos in Indiana contain important socioeconomic history. Despite their many contributions, over the years the national vitriol has been against immigrants. During the last century, this animosity was first aimed at Asians, along with southern and eastern Europeans. The Chinese Exclusion Act of 1882, together with the Immigration Act of 1924, limited the available workforce permitted to enter the country. As a result the United States, led by racist eugenics movements and the political influence of the Ku Klux Klan, shut the door on countless hard-working immigrant groups. These targeted groups—labeled "undesirables"—were from the Asian continent, Italy, Greece, Spain, and several Slavic nations.[5] The regulated quotas did not, however, apply to Latin America. For example, no cap or restrictions on Mexican immigrants existed until 1965, which meant that while the country was heavily concerned about southern and eastern Europeans, Mexicans were heavily recruited to fill America's labor needs in the first half of the twentieth century.[6] Indiana, like many other states, benefited from this policy. The continual arrival of Latinos searching for stable employment meant continuing production in its steel and automotive industries.

Hoosier Latinos depicts how Latino residents contributed to the economy at large through the creation of their own ethnic economies. Indiana Harbor entrepreneurs made cheeses for their Mexican clientele and at the same time bolstered the profits of dairy farms in Plymouth. Latino workers employed by Delco, Chrysler, and Wabash National purchased homes, paid taxes, and revitalized communities suffering from population decline. *Tamale* makers, such as María Picón, lent their culinary flavors to Indiana's palate. I witnessed this directly in Lafayette as Latino entrepreneurs revitalized previously abandoned shopping centers.[7] Mamá Inés, for instance, began in a tiny storefront in Lafayette and later branched out to three thriving locations in central Indiana. In featuring businesses and entrepreneurs in multiple areas of Indiana, *Hoosier Latinos* wonderfully narrates how Latinos subsidized the state and national economy through their labor, entrepreneurship, and purchasing power.

Contribution 4: The Pain of Discrimination

Hoosier Latinos also addresses the hard facts of pain and violence faced by many Latino residents. Irene Osorio describes the "sense of fear" created during the Great Depression when Mexican residents were "snatched and put on trains." Whether convinced or forced to leave, the Mexican community felt despised and unwanted. The bias against Latinos continues to infect the country. *Latino Heartland* (2015) speaks about the recent issues surround-

ing "driving while Mexican" to describe a heightened sense of scrutiny toward Latino drivers in certain parts of Indiana. Similarly, *Hoosier Latinos* includes an interview with Horace Piñon who recalled how his father was stopped in Muncie, Indiana, during the 1960s and "told that they didn't want to see him driving through there." This hypervigilant policing of Brown bodies, as of Black bodies, resonates with what sociologist James W. Loewen describes in his work on sundown towns, mainly outside of the South, during the twentieth century and into the twenty-first.[8] I found that even in 2011 Latino drivers still sensed a similar surveillance and prejudice toward their presence in certain Hoosier places.

Confronting this discrimination, rather than cloaking it behind the annals of time, means directly validating the memories expressed in *Hoosier Latinos*. It also commits us to abolishing the prejudice and casual racism that belittles Latino residents. Along with Horace's father, Martinez–LeGrand and Gonzales detail the experiences of Officer Robert Salinas, who was bullied in his Kokomo school as a youth. Similarly, in 2006 I worked with students at Lafayette's Jefferson High School who were mocked for being bilingual. *Hoosier Latinos* begins the much-needed task of reckoning with the prejudice that continues to view some members of society as "perpetual foreigners."[9]

One way to combat this antipathy is by shifting the way we see language. Rather than perceiving bilingualism as a detriment, we can realize that it is an incredible advantage to any community. The stories in *Hoosier Latinos* of providing bilingual services in the South Bend schools, as Greg Chávez did, or of advocating for Spanish-speaking police officers in Kokomo, as Officer Robert Salinas did, help to offset the negative assertions tied to Spanish-speakers. Moreover, how one treats newcomers, welcomes what they bring to the table, and meets them where they are linguistically can and does determine how an entire community develops. Part of meeting them where they are linguistically includes the understanding that language acquisition is not an overnight process. Also, while Latinos and other immigrants are learning English, they wish to maintain their native tongues.

Will Americans continue to divide and diminish the worth of others in increasingly dysfunctional battles for belonging? Or will we look to our neighbors and see how our wellbeing, our economy, and our success depends on what we each contribute to each other? This interdependence has always been our reality, and *Hoosier Latinos* demonstrates the possibilities available when we acknowledge the Mayan adage "*in lak'ech*"—you are my other me.[10]

Contribution 5: Latino Duality of Belonging

Embracing the advantages of bilingualism can lead toward developing an appreciation for the duality of belonging. As I referenced in *Latino Heartland* (2015), I see Indiana as a borderland, or to use the state motto—a crossroads. This metaphor speaks to the overlapping influences that gather into a collective Hoosier experience. From German bratwurst to Mexican *tamales*, the culinary and cultural scaffolding that holds up Indiana requires embracing the "in between." Rather than force one dominant mythical narrative that assumes one assimilated and fixed culture, we must open ourselves to welcoming the actual fluid nature of our identities.

Even when mail and communication were less convenient than they are today, Hoosiers found ways to stay connected to their *patrias* (homelands). The German language was present throughout Indiana generations after Germans had immigrated to the state.[11] Much like the thriving German newspapers, Indiana Harbor's *El Amigo del Hogar* newspaper maintained connections to Mexican politics while "committed to preserving *la colonia*." *Hoosier Latinos* details how *El Amigo del Hogar* and Latino mutual aid societies encouraged the youth to balance their growing attachment to the United States with a commitment to their ethnic identity. Rather than shame them into assimilating, the Mexican *colonia* of Indiana Harbor supported opportunities to sustain a healthy confidence in navigating both worlds and both identities.

This dual navigation helped during decades when redlining, an "intentional pattern of segregation," limited Latino residents in Indiana Harbor to the Block and Pennsy neighborhood. *La colonia* did not want to limit themselves to the feeling of being *arrumbados*, or cast-asides. But building a healthy, transnational identity creates an expansive sense of self that can be recalled when one is otherwise segregated and dismissed by the general society. In *Hoosier Latinos* Irene Osorio nostalgically recalls how the Mexican community had to build its own theater—*La Cuauhtémoc*—when the town's existing theater was closed to them. This story gives us a glimpse into the survival strategies and resiliency of the Latino community despite the crushing antagonism that surrounded them. As the authors note, in "preserving traditions through year-round events," Latino Hoosiers maintained a healthy cultural identity that encouraged the sense of worth necessary to prevail.

Finally, this book unearths previously overlooked moments of social activism that tie Indiana to the national Chicano Civil Rights movement in the 1960s. Carmen Velásquez's activism paralleled work done by the United Farm Workers in the Southwest. In East Chicago, students at Washington High School joined forces with *paisas* in East Los Angeles to organize collective action against unfair education practices. Young people in East Chicago and East Los Angeles balanced a duality of belonging by asserting their rights to equitable education while facing discriminatory practices. These Latino students claimed a cultural ethnic identity as a source of pride, not as a justification for inequality. Embracing a dual sense of belonging allows for the possibility of coexistence enriched by diversity.

In sum, *Hoosier Latinos* provides a perfect jumping-off point to re-examine what makes up the Hoosier experience and who Americans recognize as contributing members of society. The meticulous attention to the record and placement of Latino Hoosiers in Indiana's timeline makes this book a must read for all Indiana residents. Educators will find the rich interplay between primary materials and oral histories useful for their classroom activities. As the authors point out, *Hoosier Latinos* is only the beginning of a quest for more complete explorations of our complex past and present. I encourage teachers and community members alike to continue expanding on this collection and explore their own narratives in the history of Latinos in Indiana. As Indiana continues to welcome people from all corners of the world, its residents have the opportunity to reconcile this past with their Hoosier present and to begin building a more complex and diverse crossroads of America.

Sujey Vega
Associate Professor
Faculty Lead, American Studies
Arizona State University
September 7, 2021

Amelia Aguilera with her nephew in front of her mother's restaurant called
Bocanegra's in the Block and Pennsy neighborhood of Indiana Harbor, ca. 1950

Introduction

Indiana Historical Society Initiative Addresses Neglect of Hoosier Latino History

"The places in between allow for a duality of belonging to realities that exist somewhere between nations in carefully crafted places of comfort."[1]
　—Sujey Vega, *Latino Heartland*

In 2016 the Indiana Historical Society (IHS) initiated the Latino History Project, funded by Lilly Endowment with a grant focused on Indiana's multicultural communities. The overarching goal was to fill in the historical gap of institutionally underrepresented voices in the IHS's archives, which were founded in 1830. Although Latino communities have maintained their own rich history in Indiana for more than one hundred years, this is not thoroughly represented in archival holdings or within institutional walls. Thus, IHS made a formal commitment to this initiative, one of two specified multicultural collecting initiatives, to undo the unintentional erasure by omittance. Starting the research part of this project a half-decade before America's cultural and societal awakenings of 2020 has allowed for the publication of *Hoosier Latinos: A Century of Struggle, Service, and Success* at a most timely juncture.

When trying to understand the historic Latino, Hispanic, and more recently the Latinx experience in Indiana, researchers are met with meager archival holdings and publications that are limited by region or time period. Representational challenges are not just confined to archival materials and publications, though, for U.S.-born Latinos and Hispanics faced statistical invisibility in census reports until 1980. These roadblocks have contributed to scholarship issues which are not endemic just to Indiana, but also to the greater Midwest. When Latino history has not been overlooked, it has instead been glossed over, so that

Latinos from different countries and time periods appear as one culture. A 2015 publication about Hoosier Latino lived experiences, *Latino Heartland* by anthropologist Sujey Vega, helped frame the IHS's thought processes on how Latino history has been homogenized and misunderstood in the new millennia. In fact, Indiana has a long history with the citizens and descendants from different Latin America countries and the Caribbean—all of whom have contributed to the history, quality of life, and overall culture of the state of Indiana.

Some of Indiana's Latino and Hispanic populations are centennial communities; others have been here longer than that. Foreign-born Latinos have shown up on Indiana census rolls since the late 1800s, though the Latino community presence did not pick up until the late 1910s. World War I was the first of two global wars in which Mexico was tapped as a source of labor supply in the name of war relief. Despite showing up on census records, immigrants and consecutive generations of Latino and Hispanic Americans were not represented in state population statistics until the late twentieth century.

Regardless of the lack of written history and documented statistics of Hoosier Latinos, their communities have carved out visible spaces in the cities and rural regions of the Hoosier heartland. From *barrios* (neighborhoods) to Latino commercial business corridors, where *panaderias* (bakeries), restaurants, and *tiendas* (stores) thrive in some rural, urban, and suburban areas, Hoosier Latinos have a presence. At the same time, an almost century-old annual celebration in northwestern Indiana called *Fiestas Patrias*, Mexican Independence Day, where both the Mexican and American flags are always present, gives a prime example of the Latinos' duality of belonging. As Vega's book *Latino Heartland* explains, the power of place and belonging are both vitally important. Therefore, the addition of this publication, *Hoosier Latinos*, in Indiana's historical canon is important. By documenting the stories of people from Latin American countries who have put down stakes in Hoosier soil and contributed to the state's cultural vibrancy and economic stability, *Hoosier Latinos* cements their place in the state's history.[2]

Historical Scope

The dearth of published works about Latinos in Indiana continues to silence the long history of generations of hard-working people's contributions. Missing from the history books are narratives of their commitment to living the American Dream and participating in a democratic society, as well as stories of their ongoing struggle for equal protection under the law. Unfortunately, the brutal history of anti-Latino discrimination in America continues to paint a deficient image of Latinos past, present, and future. The IHS's work, while helping to inform and enlighten Hoosiers about the Latinos and Hispanics in their midst, also offers a different perspective on U.S. history.

The United States has a long history of turning immigration on and off, like a faucet. And as any plumber will tell you, faucets eventually leak. Over the nineteenth and twentieth centuries, Mexicans would become the most represented immigrant population in U.S. history as a result of both land grabs from Mexico and legal labor recruitment.

To begin to understand the fundamentals of Latino history in the United States is to acknowledge that it is not about Mexicans crossing the southern border, but rather that U.S.–Latino history began with the American border crossing Mexicans. Before the Treaty of Guadalupe Hidalgo in 1848, following the Mexican–American War, and subsequently in 1854 with the Gadsden Purchase, one-third of the present-day United States was inhabited by Spanish-speaking and Indigenous citizens of Mexico. Specifically, this included the present-day states of California, Texas, and parts of Colorado, Arizona, New Mexico, Utah, and Nevada. In each case, numerous Mexican citizens became residents of the United States overnight. The nine-

teenth century would end with the Spanish–American War in 1898, which caused Spain to relinquish sovereignty of Cuba, Guam, Puerto Rico, and the Philippine Islands to the United States. Many historians interpret these wars as part of an American imperialist-driven agenda, which has led to a long-lasting and complicated diplomatic relationship with Latin America.[3]

Before Hoosiers fought in the latter war, Latinos were slowly making their presence known in America's heartland. In Noblesville, Hamilton County, a Mexican *vaquero* (cowboy or cattle driver) by the nickname of "Mexican John" captivated crowds of residents in 1877 with rope lassoing tricks and by taming unmanageable horses and mules for pay. He identified himself as a "Spanish half-bre[e]d" and wore the "garb of an Indian." His presence was documented as a curiosity in local newspapers, as his visit was short-lived. Nevertheless, he remained a part of well-known local lore.[4]

In 1878 an Indianapolis photographer by the name of John Cadwallader, located at 66 East Washington Street, advertised his photographic services, requesting specific payment of "two Mexican dollars."[5] Later, a 1916 *Indianapolis News* article touted the headline "One Hundred Mexicans Live in Indianapolis," discounting them as Mexican citizens taking refuge in Indianapolis rather than as immigrants coming to live in the Hoosier capital. This article also mentioned that there was an earlier Mexican population, mainly university students, in Indiana.[6]

Throughout the 1910s Mexicans increasingly trickled into Northwest Indiana. During this time Indiana and Mexico had diplomatic relations, headquartered in Indianapolis with Colonel Russell B. Harrison serving as vice-consul. Harrison was a son and great-grandson of two U.S. presidents and had served in the Spanish–American War. Although he would threaten to publicly sever his relationship with Mexico, even publishing his resignation letter in the *Indianapolis Star* in 1916, he would serve in this position until 1927.[7]

Even less is known about Hoosiers of Spanish heritage, who are classified as Hispanic and not Latino. In unsuspecting places such as Vigo County, on the western border of Indiana, a large influx of Spanish immigrants was evident in the early 1910s. The Spanish Diaspora to the United States, let alone the Midwest, is understudied and not well documented. Mexican Americans have been inconsistently misclassified as "Spanish" in local newspapers, confusing the separate migrations of Spanish-speaking peoples.

Grasselli Chemical Company was the gravitating force of the Spanish immigration wave not only in Indiana, but also in the United States. Indiana had more than one Grasselli plant, north of Terre Haute in Vigo County and in East Chicago in Lake County. In Terre Haute the company had a zinc smelter plant. At this time zinc smelting required a specialized skillset that Spaniards brought from their homeland. A 1920 U.S. census enumeration sheet for Otter Creek Township, Vigo County, where the plant was located, listed almost every person's birthplace as Spain, with the earliest year of arrival in America noted as 1905.[8]

A reason for this unknown history could be that the Spanish presence was muted due to an upswell of Mexican and Mexican American laborers seeking work in Indiana's northwestern industrialized areas. There is evidence that a large Spanish-speaking Mexican community tends to nullify those of lesser-known origins during this period. Lesser-known histories of ethnic cultural groups and people who came to the state but did not stay are inexplicably woven into Indiana's cultural fabric.

Collecting Initiative Scope

The Latino History Project began with audio-recorded oral history interviews, the majority of which were collected in 2016 and 2017 from twenty-five individuals across Indiana. While community building on a statewide level can take years, this collecting initiative was immediately well-received by community groups and individuals. Almost 1,950 minutes of audio were recorded, resulting in 1,200 pages of transcripts that documented, through lived experience, nearly one hundred years of Latino Hoosier history together with world history. Genealogical and historical research was conducted on each participant before and after the interview and was later added to the transcript. Notations of this kind ensured that these critical narratives would stand the test of time. Additionally, paper-based ephemera and personal photos were collected that helped launch the Latino and Hispanic Heritage Collection of digital photos in 2017, located in IHS's public digital online archive. Subsequently, ten oral histories were selected to be featured in the 2018 installment of IHS's exhibition series, *Be Heard*. Profiles, audio oral history clips, and rare photos were exhibited.

The exhibition, *Be Heard: Latino Experiences in Indiana,* balanced the overarching themes of culture and contribution throughout specified time periods of American history and portrayed ethnic and cultural heritages from the Caribbean, Mexico, and South America. Each participant contributed to the betterment of Indiana on a local, regional, or statewide level.

The collecting initiative is ongoing because it is incomplete. This book's publication helps to fill in a gap documenting and publishing Latino and Hispanic experiences in Indiana, but it, too, is incomplete. Unquestionably and unintentionally are the missing voices of Afro-Latinos, Central Americans, Indigenous Latinos, and those who identify as Hispanic with heritage from Spain. Despite the challenges of preserving an expansive narrative with a complicated history, examples of the narrative and history are preserved and celebrated in this publication. Collecting this history is and will continue to be ongoing. This publication serves as a launching point for present and future historians who seek to further Latino and Hispanic scholarship in Indiana.

Nicole Martinez–LeGrand
Curator, Multicultural Collections
Indiana Historical Society, Indianapolis
September 2021

Wedding of Caesar Bonilla and Alice Gonzalez in Our Lady of Guadalupe Church in East Chicago, ca. 1950

Chapter 1

Founding of a Community, 1919–1929

The foundations of the Latino community in Indiana began in the early twentieth century with an influx of Mexicans and Mexican Americans to the northwest part of the state, specifically to Indiana Harbor, a twin city of East Chicago. This fledgling Hoosier Latino community self-identified as *la colonia*, the colony. In the wake of U.S. entry into World War I, many industries saw a massive reduction in workers as thousands were enlisted and sent overseas. They also grappled with changes to the U.S. immigration system in 1917 that drastically reduced the flow of select immigrants into the United States. Agricultural interests quickly moved to secure exemptions to the immigration laws for Mexican workers in 1918, leading to the nation's first bi-national agreement, a Mexican guest-labor program in the name of war relief. By the 1920s the Mexican and Mexican American colony of Indiana Harbor was fruitful and culturally vibrant.

New Beginnings: *La Colonia de Indiana Harbor*

Significant numbers of Latinos began arriving in Indiana in the late 1910s and early 1920s. Many of those forming the foundation of the community were recruited by industries such as steel and the railroads. Recruitment of foreign labor outside the western hemisphere was illegal; contracts could not be awarded outside of the United States; nor could jobs be advertised in foreign print publications. Companies and their labor agents, or *enganchistas*, recruited Mexican workers directly from Mexico or at various labor agencies strategically located in Texas and major U.S. cities with industries largely fueled by an immigrant workforce.[1] Those who found their way to Indiana arrived in a place that in a myriad of ways, including language, weather, and

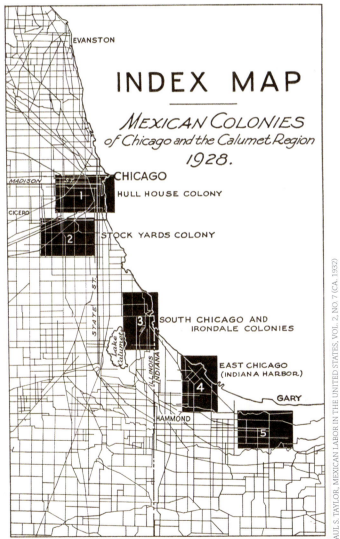

Index map of Mexican colonies of Chicago and the Calumet Region, 1928

Map of East Chicago (Indiana Harbor), 1928. The dark area closest to the Inland Steel Company is the Block and Pennsy neighborhood.

culture was fundamentally different than their homes. Many would settle in Gary and Indiana Harbor. The latter colony would settle in an area outside of Inland Steel Company's Gate No. 1, mostly in a neighborhood enclave called Block and Pennsy, short for Block and Pennsylvania Avenues. Block and Pennsy would cover 318 acres, around one-half of a square mile, with the Inland Steel Company on one end and a cement or gypsum plant on the other. Demographics of Block and Pennsy in the 1910s and 1920s would be a mix of eastern and southern Europeans, northern and southern Blacks, Mexicans, and Mexican Americans from the western United States.

Housing Conditions and Community Growth

Housing included single-family homes with basement apartments, tenements, and boarding and rooming houses, all crammed together like the densely populated areas of Chicago. This variety catered to the transient and semi-transient workers of the area's heavy industries and railroads. In some ways the Block and Pennsy neighborhood in the early half of the twentieth century, was laid out in a fashion similar to the frontier towns of the West, with numerous pool halls and saloons fueling some of the noted unruliness of the time.

Racial tensions that existed in the area increased due to the Great Steel Strike in fall 1919 and an increased recruitment of Mexican labor. Boarding and rooming houses were intentionally segregated; boarders lived within their own ethnic communities. Ownership and management of these properties might be ethnically European or Mexican, male or female. The women who ran the boarding houses were noted for being essential in retaining the much-needed Mexican laborers. Tangentially, those who managed these tenements served as *enganchistas*, labor agents or importers of foreign workers for local area industry. Thus, Block and Pennsy served as a readily available source of low-paid Mexican labor.[2]

Once the 1919 steel strike was over, Latinos continued to expand their footprint in Indiana. Growth of the early Mexican community would rapidly expand in Lake County in the 1920s. Housing stock continued to be limited and segregated. It was not uncommon for multiple boarders to be cramped into small living spaces.

The Immigration Act of 1924 further limited immigration by using a quota system, explicitly limiting immigration from southern and eastern Europe. This in effect granted Mexicans who were seeking temporary work in the United States a "non-quota" status, which increased the intensity of the recruitment of Mexican labor and the enticement, or "pull factor," for them to come. The non-quota status applied to countries located in the western hemisphere, essentially all of Latin America. There were two "push factors" aiding this growth. The first was a response to the instability of a post-revolutionary Mexico from 1910 to 1920. The second was an attempt to flee the Cristero War, an anti-Catholic uprising in the 1920s between factions within Mexico, against the Mexican government. The largest number of Mexicans would emigrate from west central Mexico, mostly from these four

SANDRA VALDÉS, INDIANA HISTORICAL SOCIETY

María del Refugio Ramírez (later Godínez) sits on the balcony of her apartment in 1926. María and her family lived at 3534 Guthrie Street in 1926. Inland Steel is visible in the background.

states: Jalisco, Michoacán, Guanajuato, and Zacatecas.[3] At the same time, the demographics of Mexican immigrants to Indiana would change from mostly single male workers (*solos*) to families and educated individuals of upper and lower middle-class backgrounds.[4]

In the early years all Mexican immigrants struggled in various ways to adjust to their new environment. Among them was a young man named Fred Maravilla. He came to the United States as a young boy in 1922 from Guarachita, Michoacán, Mexico, with his father and mother, Ignacio García Maravilla and Margarita Ruiz Ochoa. Ignacio started work for the Inland Steel Company and the New York Central Railroad. Initially, the family settled in the Indiana Harbor area but briefly moved, out of necessity, to Gary. Fred remembered his experience, stating: "I didn't know a word of English when I came to the United States. In fact, I had a very difficult time when I started school because my English was very limited. . . . I started school in 1924; I was six years old. This was right after the Teapot Dome Scandal in 1923. My dad lost his job, and he had to go work on the railroads. So we moved to Gary; we were living in a boxcar. I got to be six years old and I started school there in Gary."[5]

While the vast majority of early Latino immigrants were Mexican, not all were. Due to immigration laws that gave Latin Americans a non-quota status, Mexicans easily eclipsed Spanish-speaking immigrants who were not of Mexican origin. What we do know is that people of other Latin American countries were demographically lost in this midwestern, Spanish-speaking, Mexican-majority community. One prime example is Miguel A. Agurto, born in 1891 in Paita, Piura, Peru, who eventually lived and died in Gary, Indiana. A 1919 employment record shows him as a laborer on the Panama Canal, working for 17 cents an hour (in 2021, $2.55 USD).[6] He spent his twenties helping to build the canal, which cuts through the Central American country of Panama. The canal revolutionized trade and logistics by connecting the Atlantic and Pacific Oceans. Miguel's employment at the Panama Canal spanned from working on the railroad to the docks in the Cristóbal Canal Zone (Port of Colón). How, when, and why he made the jump from Panama to Indiana is a bit of a mystery. What we do know is that the U.S. Steel Corporation and its subsidiary, Universal Atlas Cement Company, provided both the steel and a type of cement called portland cement needed to build and maintain this waterway. U.S. Steel had plants in Indiana and other U.S. states. At one time it was the largest steel producer in the world. It was not uncommon for labor agents in Panama to be working to recruit foreign labor for steel plants throughout the United States. Miguel appears

in the Gary City Directory in 1929 and is employed as a steelworker. But a customs declaration form from 1924 shows that he is there even earlier in the decade. This customs form was for a doll he shipped from Gary to Panama, a doll likely sent to family he left behind there.[7]

The work found by the early Latino immigrants, such as the Maravillas and Miguel Agurto, in the growing industrial center of Northwest Indiana was most of all in the steel industry. Over the years, Latinos formed a major part of the workforce at U.S. Steel, Inland Steel, and other mills around the state. Increasingly they also contributed to union organizing efforts, including a strike in May 1937 when union leaders noted that three-fourths of those on the picket line were Latino.[8]

Mexican Commerce in Indiana

The rapid growth of the Mexican population in Indiana Harbor during the 1920s brought the development of many Mexican-owned and operated businesses, approximately

Connie Figueroa, daughter of Francisco and Consuelo Figueroa, leans outside of a window directly above the Figueroa Print Shop, which her family owned, on Deodar Street, Indiana Harbor, ca. 1940s.

seventy of them by 1928.[9] One of the most successful was *El Popular.* Vicente F. Garza, locally known as V. F. Garza, founded the food brand in Indiana sometime between 1925 and 1927. Initially, *El Popular* sold Mexican-style cheese and chocolate, the latter a key ingredient in the Mexican sauce called *mole.* The company also incorporated chorizo, a type of pork sausage, into their offerings. Chorizo is a key staple that has sustained *El Popular* for almost one hundred years. Today the company is the oldest Latino-owned company in Indiana.

Another early Indiana business is the Figueroa family's print shop. The Figueroas worked closely with the Garza family, printing paper wrappers for their company's products. Francisco and Consuelo Figueroa immigrated from Mexico in the early 1920s. Francisco would be first, arriving in 1923 with his brother, Benjamín. Later he would return to Mexico and bring his nineteen-year-old bride to Indiana Harbor. The brothers with Consuelo owned and operated the print shop in their family name, the Figueroa Print Shop. More important, Francisco owned the Deodar Street apartment building in which their storefront shop was located. In partnership with his mutual aid society *Círculo de Obrero Católicos San José,* Francisco began publishing a newspaper called *El Amigo del Hogar* (Friend of the Home) in 1925. It was the first Spanish-language paper in Indiana and was distributed weekly until the early 1930s.

The newspaper covered the political happenings of Mexico, reviews on literature, and most of all served by maintaining and preserving the cultural awareness of *la colonia,* Indiana Harbor. *El Popular* and the Figueroa Print Shop would not be the only Mexican owned and operated businesses of Indiana Harbor. By the end of the 1920s, the Latino community in Indiana Harbor would have twenty pool halls, ten restaurants, seven barbershops and grocers, three tailors and bakeries, and an ice cream factory, to name a few.[10]

Cultural and Mutual Aid Societies

As a fledgling community with little political or social power, Latinos in the early years struggled with poverty, discrimination, cultural isolation, and the internal social stratification of class. Despite these elements, community members banded together and found strength through the mutual love of their homeland. Not only would the community grow rapidly during the 1920s, but also during this decade the Hoosier Latino community in Indiana Harbor would experience the rapid growth of a social hierarchy through the development of cultural societies. The most culturally vibrant period occurred from 1923 to 1929.

Latinos in Indiana remained committed to preserving their national traditions in *la colonia* by continuing to observe a certain social hierarchy that the Mexican Revolution had sought to destroy. They did this by developing and participating in certain *mutualistas,* mutual aid, and cultural societies. By 1929 there were a total of twelve societies, most of them cultural societies, including: *Sociedad Pro Patria* (est. 1922, disbanded 1923), *Sociedad Mutualista Benito Juárez* (est. 1924), *Círculo de Obreros Católicos San José* (est. 1924), *Sociedad Cuauhtémoc* (est. 1925), *Sociedad Mutualista José María Morelos* (est. 1926), *Sociedad Feminina Mexicana,* associated with *Sociedad Benito Juárez* (est. 1928), *Club de los 13, Club Deportivo International* (est. 1929), and *Tesoro del Hogar* (est. 1929).[11] The cultural societies were formed to advance the community by preserving traditions through year-round events such as bazaars, *jamaicas,* or festivals, dances, and vaudeville

SANDRA VALDÉS, INDIANA HISTORICAL SOCIETY

Mexican American youth sit on a park bench in Washington Park in Indiana Harbor in East Chicago during the 1920s. María del Refugio Ramírez is sitting with her boyfriend, Rafael Martínez Godínez, on the far right.

performances. The most important events occurred during the month of September with the patriotic activities of *Fiestas Patrias*.

There were also events that helped maintain social classes that were geared toward cultural refinement. Most notably the group *Círculo de Obreros Católicos San José* maintained a predilection toward the arts. It had its own theater group, *El Cuadro Dramático*, that was directed by a former professional actor from Mexico City. Under his direction the theater group performed several plays a year, keeping up with cosmopolitan productions that were performed in Mexico City. Furthermore, they hosted an exhibition of artwork by Mexican artist Alfaro Siqueiros who was on the cusp of achieving international fame.[12]

While the social groups were created to preserve cultural heritage, *mutualistas* were created to maintain the overall health of the community in the form of advocacy. *Mutualistas* advocated on behalf of *la colonia* by providing sick ben-efits, insurance needs, and legal protections. Those mutual aid societies were: *Hijos de México* (est. 1928), *Comisión Honorífica* (est. 1926), *Cruz Azul* (est. ca. 1921), and *Sociedad Santa Cruz* (est. 1929).[13]

One of the long-lasting vestiges of these groups that exists to this day is the annual *Fiestas Patrias* events and parade. Early accounts of the celebration of *Fiestas Patrias* or Mexican Independence Day, can be traced as far back as 1923. Newspaper accounts from the time estimated that the Mexican population of Indiana Harbor was anywhere from 2,000 to 3,000. *Fiestas Patrias* was celebrated in mid-September. Mexican Independence Day is September 16, but some celebrations began the night before. In 1924 Indiana Harbor's National Hall was the location of a banquet with guest of honor, G. Luis Lupian, the Mexican consul in Chicago. The *Hammond* (Indiana) *Times* noted that the banquet was festively and patriotically decorated in red, white, and green bunting, the national colors of Mexico.

To illustrate appreciation for their newfound homeland, there was also decorative bunting in red, white, and blue. Reflecting this duality would be a fixture in all of their celebrations for generations.[14]

In addition to the banquet, dances, a community festival, and musical events took place over a few days. While 1923 is the earliest report of a parade being part of the festivities, the most noted and celebrated tradition of crowning a *Fiestas Patrias* queen did not come until 1926. This honor was first bestowed upon twenty-one-year-old María del Refugio Ramírez (later Godínez) at a ceremony in Auditorium Hall the Wednesday before the Thursday parade. The *Hammond Times* misidentified Miss Ramírez as "Miss Martínez."[15] The tradition of the *Fiestas Patrias* parade and the nomination of a festival queen exists to this day. In its history, the parade has only been halted during the years the U.S. was involved in World War II, the week following the September 11th terrorist attacks in 2001, and in response to the 2020 and 2021 COVID-19 global pandemic.

SANDRA VALDÉS, INDIANA HISTORICAL SOCIETY

Studio portrait of María del Refugio Ramírez as Fiestas Patrias *queen, 1926. Although the first-recorded* Fiestas Patrias *parade in Indiana Harbor took place in 1923, the first nomination of a queen was in 1926. María was that queen.*

Parishioners line up to form a procession for the inaugural mass of Our Lady of Guadalupe Catholic Church in its new location on Deodar Street, Indiana Harbor, in 1940.

Our Lady of Guadalupe Church

As mentioned above, the second driving force of emigration from Mexico into the United States was *La Cristiada* (the Cristero War), brought on partially by a perceived anti-Catholic and anti-clergy movement in post-revolutionary Mexico. After the start of the Mexican Revolution in 1910, the Mexican Constitution was amended with several articles in 1917 to reduce the influence of the Vatican and the Roman Catholic Church in Mexico. This included the suppression and later suspension of public displays of faith, which were central to Mexican celebrations and traditions. For many Mexicans this would be the sole impetus to leave their homeland—religious freedom.

With this impetus, along with the formation of both cultural and mutual aid societies, *la colonia* quickly built the framework to raise the funds needed for a Latino church.

Much like the rooming and boarding houses of the Indiana Harbor area, churches were also ethnically segregated. Practicing Latino Catholics found Father Octavio Zavatta, an Italian priest who spoke Spanish and offered services in the basement of Saint Demetrius Romanian Catholic Church at 138th and Butternut Streets. Fundraising efforts began between 1925 and 1926 and were initially overseen by *Círculo de Obreros Católicos San José*. Money was raised through fundraisers and proceeds from festivals. Other fundraising groups dedicated to the church would develop, such as *Oracíon de la Apostaldo*. Among those who would be members of and contributors to the church via the *Apostaldo* group was the Reyes family. José Reyes and his wife, María Picón Reyes, settled in Indiana Harbor with their daughter, María de Jesús, in 1922. María Picón would be a fundraiser and lifetime member of the *Apostaldo* group.

By 1926 the Latino community members were able to purchase a plot of land for their church at 3855 Pennsylvania Avenue, in the Block and Pennsy neighborhood of Indiana Harbor. A modest wood structure that could seat two hundred individuals was completed by 1927 and dedicated to *La Nuestra Señora de Guadalupe*, Our Lady of Guadalupe, the Patroness of the Americas. This would be the first recorded Latino Roman Catholic Church in the state of Indiana.[16] The church was more than a place of worship; it was an anchor institution that supported, advocated for, and grew with *la colonia*. For instance, in 1929 Bishop Francis Noll instructed the nearby Our Lady of Victory missionary nuns to work with the families of Indiana Harbor.[17]

In 1939 the church partially burned down in an accidental, yet devastating fire. Once again, the community banded together, raising the funds to rebuild a larger church on the same site. Before the fire the local Black community was welcomed at the Pennsylvania Avenue church and was offered its own select times to hold services. However, soon after rebuilding the church, the Latinos realized that their numbers were already outgrowing the new building. They then purchased a land plot at 3520 Deodar Street and set forth plans to build a $35,000 (in 2021, $647,027) brick church that doubled capacity for the growing congregation. The Pennsylvania Avenue church was renamed Saint Jude and served as the first Black Roman Catholic Church in Indiana Harbor. On *Fiestas Patrias* weekend in 1940, Mass was celebrated for one last time on Pennsylvania Avenue and concluded with a ten-block procession with a statue of Our Lady of Guadalupe to *la colonia's* new parish home.[18]

The founding era of Latinos in Indiana was integral in setting down core institutions, traditions, and patterns of settlement, many of which remain in the early twenty-first century. As Latinos continue to grow in population and move into new areas of the state, these roots remain vitally important in understanding Hoosier Latino story.

History in Their Own Words: Stories from the Founding of a Community

The interview excerpts found at the end of each chapter of this book are taken from recorded oral interviews conducted by Nicole Martinez–LeGrand for the Indiana Historical Society. After the brief introduction for each set of interview excerpts, the date of the interview and the age of the individual at the time of the interview are given.

The audio recordings were transcribed by Data Logistics Control, Incorporated. Many of them were then audited by historian Nancy M. Germano. If an interview was audited, credit will be given to Germano along with the date of the interview.

All transcripts were lightly edited for accuracy by Martinez–LeGrand. They were lightly edited again by the IHS Press for clarity for this book. The original interview recordings and the transcriptions are available in IHS's William Henry Smith Memorial Library.

Fred Maravilla

Fred moved to Indiana Harbor as a toddler. He served as one of the team managers for the *Gallinas* womens baseball team after graduating from Washington High School in East Chicago, Indiana. After serving in the European theater during World War II, he returned to Northwest Indiana to his wife, Sabina "Sophie" and young daughter. He utilized the GI Bill to earn bachelor's and master's degrees. Fred spent his career as a high school Spanish teacher and local area college instructor. His interview explores his experiences immigrating to the United States and the

This border crossing card documents Frederick R. Maravilla and his parents' entry into the United States on Friday, May 19, 1922. (Manifest, U.S. Department of Labor, Immigration Service, Mexican Border District form for Ignacio Maravilla, U.S. Border Crossings from Mexico to U.S., 1895–1964, A3437, Laredo, Texas, 1903–1955, NARA Roll 076, Ancestry)

*Joseph (seated)
and Frederick Mara-
villa in outfits made
by their mother,
Margarita Ruiz
Maravilla, 1923*

conditions of Indiana Harbor as a young child. This excerpt, however, deals primarily with Inland Steel.

Date of interview: September 24, 2016 | Age at time of interview: 98 years

Fred Maravilla on Coming to Indiana: Indiana Harbor and the Inland Steel Company

FM: *My father had come to the United States in 1919 with three brothers, an older brother named Cándido. My father was next in line in age, and another brother José, and then a younger brother who was sixteen years old, Abel. They came up the regular way, undocumented, worked in the cotton fields and then on the railroads. While they were working on the railroads they were hired by the representatives from the Inland Steel Company in Indiana Harbor, in Indiana which is really*

East Chicago.[19] At the time Indiana Harbor had a post office separate from East Chicago, but Indiana Harbor was a part of Chicago.

But they were hired and taken to Chicago by train and then put on boats and then taken into the mill on the lake because at the time the steel industry was in the national strike.[20] I think it was the Workers of The World at the time that had called a national strike.[21] And it's said that they were communist oriented. . . . But anyhow, they were quartered in the mill, they had a commissary for them to eat, and they had cots for them to sleep, and the mill kept producing and eventually the strike fizzled. . . . So our parents actually, who worked in the mill at the time, were "scabs" and they continued to work in the mill for two years.[22] My father and my uncle Carl went back, as well as Uncle Joe, also later, and brought back their families. So we entered the United States in May of 1922.[23]

Now my father didn't have enough money to come all the way to Indiana Harbor, and I remember that we were in Saint Louis, Missouri, at the depot. And my father was in the quandary what to do—whether to stay and look for work there—and we would remain in the depot there for a long, long time. And a lady who I suppose was a member of the Traveler's Assistance Society, who spoke some Spanish, inquired why we were [there] so long and that if we had taken any trains.[24] And my father explained that he had run out of money. And so she sent a telegram to my uncle Cándido who was already working in the mill again, and she took us to a restaurant, fed us, and rented a room for us to stay overnight. And the following day we got the money by telegraph from my uncle Cándido and continued the trip to Indiana Harbor. . . ."

My father got his job and we—when we got to Indiana Harbor there were no accommodations for us. We lived for several months in the garage behind the apartment house that my uncle Cándido [lived in]. My uncle Cándido and two neighbors that became very good friends to us, the Torres family and the Dávalos family, were already there. My uncle after three or four months left Inland to work at the Wisconsin Steel Works in South Deering, Illinois, and when his apartment became vacant, we moved in. But for several months we slept on the concrete floor in the empty garage. . . .

My father had bought the [mattress] ticks and filled them with straw and we slept on the floor and we had no toilet facilities. We had a bed pan that we would do our duty and then in the morning take it to my uncle's apartment and use his toilet to get rid of the waste. And we started off with—for a table, my father found a large crate, wooden crate and orange boxes for chairs. It was really tough but we managed."

Edward Medina

Edward Medina was born in the Mexican community of Northwest Indiana and later served in the U.S. Army. He spent his career in the steel industry and as a studio and community photographer, submitting photos for the newspaper *Latin Times*. In the following interview excerpts he discusses his grandparents and parents' immigration to Indiana and the founding years of Our Lady of Guadalupe Catholic Church.

Date of interview: September 1, 2016 | Age at time of interview: 86 years

Coming to Indiana Harbor

EM: *My parents were, Father was Antonio Medina, from Mexico, from the State of Jalisco.[25] My mother was María de Jesús Reyes, also from Mexico. . . .[26] They came and they were married*

in East Chicago, Indiana. . . .[27] I know that my father was working on the railroad and he worked all the way up to, migrated down from Texas, all the way up to Springfield, Illinois, and then he heard about the steel mills factories, so he came up this way. I don't know too much about my mother's parents, but they were, I know that my grandfather was working in the steel mills and this is where [Indiana Harbor] they [parents] met, this is where they got married. . . . Mostly one of the main reasons I understood for them [his grandparents] to break away from Mexico was because of the religious persecution that was going on in Mexico, so they came up this way. . . .[28]

A typical residential neighbourhood with a lot of a different type of ethnic people.[29] East Chicago and Indiana Harbor was a little melting pot with all different types of nationalities—but a lot of industry. Mainly there were two big steel mills, the Inland Steel Company and the Youngstown Sheet and Tube Company.[30]

Latinos had a tendency to kind of try to be a little bit clannish because of the, they wanted to be close to each other or because they were, this is where the places for them to rent were available. And usually was all close to the mill. There was

Children of Antonio Medina and María de Jesús (Reyes) Medina. From left to right: María Engracia (Grace) Eduardo (Edward), Josefina (Josie), and María Magdalena (Malena) Medina. This photo was taken in Indiana Harbor in the 1930s.

also a lot of oil refineries around there, but the majority of the people were working in the steel mills and not so much in the oil refinery. . . .

Back in my times, I would say 99 percent were Mexicans of Mexican [national] extraction. Not until later on, during the World War II, they started to get more, or later people from Puerto Rican people and other central American countries.

Our Lady of Guadalupe Church

EM: *It [Our Lady of Guadalupe church] was first located on the far east end of Pennsylvania Avenue, and then they bought some property over on Deodar Street where they built the church there. So then the parish moved over here to Deodar Street. The old church then became Saint Jude's Church, but it was still a Catholic church. It was serving those people that were over in that area and then this new one, Our Lady of Guadalupe on Deodar Street, where they then built the third church right there. . . .*

Nicole Martinez–LeGrand (NML): The third version of Our Lady of Guadalupe church?

EM: *Right.*

NML: Okay. Still on Deodar Street?

EM: *Still on Deodar. . . . It's still there today.*

NML: So that's where you learned how to type from the French priest, and you were an altar boy there. So you had a lot of close ties. So did you have a close relationship with the church as an adult?

EM: *Not too much after that because I got tied up working in the mill and working on my house, but I always went to church on Sundays.*

NML: That's good. So were any of your family members like your mother, your grandmother, and your sisters, were they all members of the same church?

EM: *Oh yes, well, not my sisters that much. My grandmother, my maternal grandmother, María Picón Reyes, that woman had all kind of comadres all over the place. . . .*[31] *She was the head of all different kind of religious groups, like there was the Apostleship of Prayer, a group that she belonged to. She also belonged to the, what was it called? I forget the name—Las Guadalupanas. . . . She was dues collector, going from house to house to collect dues.*

NML: Was she a good fundraiser?

EM: *I guess so.*

NML: Well, she was successful; the church is still here today.

EM: *I remember one thing about her—that she was a very good hot tamale maker. The church would have their little fiestas, and everybody would be making their own stuff to contribute, and whatever they got they would they donate that to the church. And I remember on several occasions, back when we were at the old church, the one on Pennsy, they would have the*

Reyes Family, from left to right: María Picón Reyes, her husband José Reyes, and teenage daughter María de Jesús Reyes. This photo was taken in Indiana Harbor, ca. 1923.

fiesta and the ladies would come, some would have pozole, *some would have* menudo. . . .[32]

Okay, we're talking back in the old, old church, the one that was located on Pennsylvania Avenue. I remember that some of the ladies were upset with her. Why they would get upset with her is because the other ladies would get there on time, they would take all the food there and everything else, but María Picón was always late, because she was always, she would, and a lot of these people were waiting for her, would wait for María Picón to get here with her tamales *because they wanted her* tamales*: "Yeah, but somebody else has* tamales*."*

"Yeah, but I know, but we are waiting for María Picón." That happens a few times and some people just got offended and got hurt because of the fact that they were good. . . . Yeah, and I remember that we lived about three blocks down the street on Pennsylvania, and she would make her tamales *in these big pots and would put them on a little wagon, and we would pull the wagon all the way down the street, all the way to church.*

Sandra Valdés

Sandra Valdés is the child of Mexican immigrants who helped found the Mexican community in Indiana. Her parents would meet in Indiana Harbor in the 1920s but would separate and reconnect when her father was on a visit to Mexico in the 1940s. They would marry in Mexico and return to Indiana Harbor together. Sandra was born in Indiana Harbor and grew up to have a successful career as an education and human resources professional. In this interview excerpt she discusses her mother, María del Refugio Ramírez (later Godínez), the inaugural queen of the *Fiestas Patrias* parade in Indiana Harbor, a tradition that exists today.

Date of interview: November 14, 2017 | Age at time of interview: 69 years | Interview transcript audited by Nancy M. Germano (2017–18)

Sandra Valdés on the First *Fiestas Patrias* Queen

SV: *She [her mother] told me that Mr. José Anguiano—he went to her house—to her home—he spoke to my grandmother.[33] He said, "Please, Mrs. Ramírez," or "Señora, please let Cuca—" because they used to call her—they called her Cuca. . . . "Please, we want her as queen for the festivities." And my grandmother said no. . . . But that Señor Anguiano he's over there—"Please, please," you know, "we want her as queen." So, finally, they convinced her, and that's why.*

NML: So, and that was what—in 1926?

SV: *Yeah, in '26.*

NML: So, literally, she was, probably, the very first *Fiestas Patrias* queen.

SV: *I think so. She said that she was.*

NML: Well, I think back—and so now—but before it was probably you were just, kind of, suggested to be the queen.[34]

SV: *Yeah. . . .*

NML: Interesting. So you brought me two beautiful photos: one, your mother as queen with all of the, I guess, kind of—

SV: *The court. (Laughs)*

NML: Yeah, the court. So there's two women and three men, and then, the one with the—

SV: *The float.*

NML: The float—the cars, so it's all, probably, like a—I don't know—early Model-T convertible, and it's just covered in beautiful white flowers. Then your mother's sitting on top. So there's all these different men. So you pointed out that your father is in this photo.

SV: *No, no, no, no—no, the* chambelán *[escort] was that one.*[35]

NML: Oh, Frederico—the guy with the hat [Conrado Calderón].[36]

SV: *The short one. (Laughs)*

Irene Osorio

Irene Osorio's father and mother, Francisco and Consuelo Figueroa, were the owners of the Figueroa Print Shop, which published newspapers in the 1920s and late twentieth century for the Latino community in Indiana Harbor. Her father was a member of *Círculo de Obreros San José,* which oversaw the production of *El Amigo del Hogar,* Indiana's first Spanish language newspaper in Indiana. Irene grew up and worked in education at Indiana University Northwest and Valparaiso University, as well as in human resources at Inland Steel, Progressive Rail, and Corn Products (now called Ingredion). In this interview excerpt she discusses the establishment of her family's printshop and the early Mexican *colonia.*

SANDRA VALDÉS, INDIANA HISTORICAL SOCIETY

SANDRA VALDÉS, INDIANA HISTORICAL SOCIETY

Left: Portrait of María del Refugio Ramírez, ca. 1920s; Right: Portrait of Rafael Martínez Godínez. Rafael was María del Refugio's boyfriend before her crowning as the Fiestas Patrias queen. They broke up and rekindled their romance in Mexico, where they later married. The couple returned to Indiana Harbor in the early 1940s.

Date of interview: July 28, 2017 | Age at time of interview: 68 years | Interview transcript audited by Nancy M. Germano (2017–18)

Irene Osario on Figueroa Printshop and Newspaper

IO: *I don't know how he knew about the printing business. I believe—what they wanted to do—the brothers, Benjamín and Carlos, and my father, Francisco—what they wanted was to have a way to connect with the Hispanic community that was growing there in Indiana Harbor and to share information and knowledge, and one of the best ways to do that was in print.*[37] *They might have just known this because of their experiences in Mexico. So—but I don't know how they came about it or how they got the equipment—the press itself. I know that we do have—my son has in his garage—the first printing press that my father had, and it's about table-size, and it's heavy!*

NML: It's probably iron.

IO: *Yes, it is, and you do everything by hand, and it had little rollers—got a little round wheel at the top where you would put the ink and the roller would go up and get it, and then you'd roll over the print and then press the paper on it. It was pretty labor intensive. And from there, of course, when they got the newspaper together,* El Amigo del Hogar, *and other things that they did. They did a lot of bartering with the other little businesses in the neighborhood because, again, finances—and try to help each other out. And I remember my mom saying that*

my dad would print wrapping paper for the Garzas, like for their chocolates.

NML: Oh, the V. F. Garza family.[38]

IO: *Um-hm. The chocolates or the cheese—whatever they were making, and then Mr. Garza would then give my father cheese and chocolate (laughs) for the papers that he printed and wrapped for him. And they became godparents to each other's children. They lived not too far from each other—a couple of houses down. And the same thing happened with, you know, people, different stores that he would print different things for them, and they would in exchange give food or things of that nature. . . .*

NML: So their newspaper, *El Amigo del Hogar,* translates "A Friend in the Home."

IO: *Friend of the Home.*

NML: Oh, *Friend of the Home.* And so, how long did the newspaper stay in operation?

IO: *Definitely a good five years that I'm aware of—'25 to like '30. And again, right with the Depression all of that kind of stopped because—the '28, '29—the Depression and things getting tough, and—and then the brothers leaving—because the brothers were the, you know, the editors, the publishers, the writers, and that sort of thing. But they were pretty good with the newspaper. They had people that advertised in it—the Garzas (laughs). . . .*

NML: So what would they report on—just local happenings in East Chicago? Or would they report on things that were happening in Mexico, post the revolution?

IO: *Definitely Mexico as well. It was news for the community from home to also, sort of, maintain cultures. What—they wanted the people to continue speaking Spanish, to be proud of who they were and where they came from. It was a—the paper came as a result of a group of men who were called* Los Obreros de San José, *so the—and* Santo—*Saint Joseph is the patron of workers, so consequently the name* Los Obreros de San José, *and then (pauses)—it was* Círculo de Obreros de San José, *so it's a circle of workers and patron saint, San José—and then the* Friend of the Home *came about as a result. And they tried to do a lot of things to maintain the culture. For example, they had—my mom would tell stories of them putting on plays. And different people in the community would partake in that, and they'd kind of dress up in the costumes, and they'd perform skits and talent shows and things of that nature. I believe part of it was a way to help them stay in touch with what it was that they knew in Mexico because up here they weren't really allowed to go to theaters or to participate in—you know, they were expected to stay in their little enclave.*

NML: Their little *colonia*.

IO: *Um-hm.*

Richard Garza on His Father, V. F. Garza

Richard Garza was the second son born of a set of twins to Ana and Vicente Flores "V. F." Garza, Mexican immigrants. Richard's twin brother died from pneumonia in infancy. Vicente would be one of the earliest and most well-known importers of Mexican goods and a producer of chocolate, cheese, and chorizo in Indiana Harbor. Born in Nuevo León, Mexico, he had worked and been a proprietor of a small candy store in Texas before coming to Indiana. Vicente's wife, Ana, would also contribute with her family's chorizo recipe, which would sustain their family business, *El Popular*, through to the present day. *El Popular* is the oldest Latino owned business in Indiana.

Date of interview: March 4, 2020 | Age at time of interview: 90

Crossing from Mexico into the United States

RG: *Well, he never used Flores. . . . When you cross the border, when my dad crossed the border, he wouldn't have put it,*

Francisco Figueroa and Consuelo Figueroa, ca. 1920s

Vicente Garza Flores. They said he couldn't do it. Then he used the initial, Flores, as an initial. V. F. out of circumstance.

Early Indiana Harbor

RG: *It was all kind of. . . . Deodar was very mixed neighborhood. . . . Most of the Mexican people were in Block and Pennsy. . . . There were a lot of Mexicans, but they were isolated throughout the city. We live[d] on Deodar most of the time."*

My wife's family, they were here in the '20s. And they were very close to a Greek grocery store. And she said they used to make hot sauce and some other things. . . . The Greek store sold to a lot of people. But she cooked at home.

Beginnings of a Business

RG: *His [father's] reason to get into the food business, the need of the Mexican food that was there. The need was there. He fulfilled the need for the Mexican population. Not for the Anglos, but for the Mexican people.*

We had very little competition. Because the people that were here, were so few. And there wasn't enough people to make a living. As the population grew, then all of a sudden, wholesalers start, sprouted out, and people specializing in just cheese, just chorizio. La Preferida didn't even exist. Nobody existed. My dad was the first and only.

I think chocolate was the first item. . . . Next one was cheese and then chorizo. . . . Ok, at first he made his own from milk.

Vicente F. Garza (bottom right with glasses) stands next to his car decorated as a float for the Fiestas Patrias parade in 1928. The float advertises his business, El Popular, *located at 3506 Deodar Street, Indiana Harbor.*

Just a local dairy factory in Highland, Indiana. There was a dairy. And then he started, from them—the curd. They would curdle the milk. And then they would put them in cans. And then they would take them and break it down to process it further. And make the cheese out of it. The last one was from Plymouth, Indiana, Slasher Brothers. That dairy made everything. Pretty soon they started to specializing, dropping this, dropping that. . . . everyone started specializing. . . . and that was the end of that.

Remembering His Father, V. F. Garza

RG: *He used to tell people, everyone asked—"What is the 'F' for?" He would say, "Feo (ugly)." [Laughs]. . . . My dad had a real good sense of humor. . . . He was very upbeat in his nature. . . . My dad was very, very happy, that was his being, just the way he was. . . . He paid me. . . . In fact he taught me, he says, "Rich, what you should do, is whatever you earn, is give your mother something, save something and spend the rest any way you want. But never spend more than you make." That stuck in my mind since I was very, very young.*

VELÁSQUEZ FAMILY, INDIANA HISTORICAL SOCIETY

Family photo of Carmen and Albert Velásquez with their children at their home in Fairmount, Indiana, 1966

Chapter 2

Era of Tumultuous Growth, 1929–1969

From the stock market crash in October 1929 to the start of the Chicano Civil Rights Movement in the 1960s, the Latino community in Indiana experienced a lot of change—change in the density of the Latino population after the Mexican repatriation of the 1930s as well as cultural diversity after World War II. Additionally, the Bracero guest worker program, which was initiated under a series of bi-national farm labor agreements between the United States and Mexico in 1942, began bringing Latinos from Mexico and the western states to the Midwest. In turn, Latinos founded more communities throughout Indiana. By the end of this era, the Latino population in the state was nearing one percent of the population and continuing in an upward trajectory.

1929–1939: Discrimination, Deportation, and Faith

Discrimination against Latinos in Indiana had long been a reality, particularly where their population was numerous, as in Northwest Indiana. Latinos found discrimination in housing; different ethnic groups were segregated not only by choice but also because they were not allowed to rent outside of their own neighborhoods. Hotels and movie theaters often refused service to Latinos. Even in death some Latinos faced hostility, as a cemetery in Gary was segregated during the 1920s. Latinos also suffered harsh and prejudicial treatment by police, including illegal searches. As a result, in 1931 investigators for the Wickersham Commission examined police treatment of the Mexican population in both Indiana Harbor and Gary, Indiana.[1] Worse yet, during the Great Depression, Mexicans became a central focus of nativist sentiment. A national program of deportation and coerced repatriation, encouraged by federal policy

and primarily executed at the local level, led to hundreds of thousands of Mexican immigrants and Mexican Americans—many U.S. citizens—being expelled from the United States. The Gary International Institute quoted one female repatriate as stating, "'This is my country but after the way we have been treated I hope never to see it again. . . . As long as my father was working and spending his money in Gary stores, paying taxes, and supporting us, it was all right, but now we have found we can't get justice here.'"[2]

Many of those forced to leave were from Indiana. In fact, the midwestern states of Indiana, Illinois, and Michigan produced an outsized share of repatriates, representing an estimated 10.5 percent of all those who were expelled in this period.[3] By 1930 the U.S. census reported that there were 9,642 Mexicans living in Indiana. A little over 9,000 of them lived in Lake County, primarily in Indiana Harbor and Gary. Repatriation efforts began in the early 1930s; by 1932 a total of 3,300 Mexican residents from East Chicago and Gary had been repatriated to Mexico. Local newspapers widely publicized this as a humanitarian relief program due to unemployment and the concern that local Mexicans were at risk of becoming public charges. Some, but not all, of those repatriated were on poor relief.[4]

Funding for transportation back to Mexico had to be provided at the local level. In Lake County the Township Trustee Office, community trust, and American Legion helped with the needed financial support. Special arrangements and a fixed train fare were put in place to help with voluntary, and later, coerced repatriation. The train fare charity rate to Mexico was $24.00, but a special subsidized railroad fare for this program was set at $15.00 for adults and $7.50 for a half fare, presumably for children.

COLONY HERE REDUCED TO LOW FIGURE

Only 3,500 Mexicans Left in Twin City After Big Exodus

Two hundred and sixty persons, for the most part contained in family groups, filled a nine-car train at the Pennsylvania depot at Indiana Harbor yesterday and started on their long journey back to Mexico and the farms they left to seek wealth in the mills here. This is the third train load of Mexicans to be returned to their native country from the Twin City and further relieves the poor relief burden. It is estimated now that there are only 3,500 Mexicans in the colony here which two years ago approached 6,000.

Tragedy and comedy were intermingled as some of the people were sad at leaving their homes here, where their children were given equal rights with all for an education and where they had made friends and in many cases were leaving relatives. Some of the family groups had lived here for many years and their almost grown children had never lived anywhere but in Indiana Harbor.

Others were happy that they were returning to Mexico where their training in mills and factories and schools would help them to secure better positions than in this country.

The train was held a full hour over time and moved from the local depot at 1 o'clock, because of the careful check of all of the passengers, and the efforts made by relief agencies to see that each car was rationed and comforts for babies were provided.

Thousands of people were attracted by the embarkation but were barred from the sides of the train, as relief workers checked the passengers and their parcels of trinkets and food.

Some excitement was added when a burning cigarette caught fire to steps of one of the cars, and a red-haired woman with the map of Old Erin on her face, leaned from a car and in shrill Mexican directed the fire fighters. She was a native Mexican and Cortez must have had some Irishman among his fighting men.

The train, which is proceeding under the personal direction of Paul Kelly of the Emergency Relief association, will proceed directly to the Mexican border at Laredo, where the people will be turned over to the Mexican government. The cars were sealed here and moved to the Wabash tracks where they were whisked away by a waiting engine.

Seated in specially designated train cars, Latinos departed from the Pennsylvania Avenue Depot in Indiana Harbor and went directly to Laredo, Texas. It was there that an official from the Mexican government would assist them for the last leg of their journey.[5] This coerced repatriation program was aimed both at the many *solos,* the single male workers of the area, and at families. A 1932 Lake County Unemployment Relief Report states that there were 250 Mexican children in East Chicago public schools. In 1928, before the start of the Great Depression, there had been 465 elementary school children of Mexican descent. Some, if not most, were U.S. citizens by birth. The elementary schools that they attended were Lincoln, Field, Riley, Garfield, and Harrison.[6] Deportation of nearly half these children is stated to have saved $21,000 annually that would be good "for years to come."[7]

The Latinos left behind faced discrimination in hiring practices and reduced access to social resources. Nevertheless, the community persisted, and many of the deported children would later return to the United States and Indiana Harbor as young adults. Those who remained would be sustained by the missionary catechists of Our Lady of Guadalupe church, who would provide support both spiritually and materially. The church itself continued to be a developmental force of the Mexican *colonia*. For example, both Fred Maravilla and Edward Medina credited the missionary priests and nuns of Our Lady of Guadalupe church for their high school instruction on how to use a typewriter, a profitable skill and an uncommon one for men of that time.

During the depression, the missionaries turned their focus to the youth in the community, meeting their recreational needs through the Catholic Youth Organization (CYO). They sponsored men's and women's baseball teams, as baseball had already established roots in this community with teams dating back to the late 1920s.[8] It was during this turbulent time that baseball would help cement a sense of belonging in *la colonia's* early Indiana Harbor residents, the assurance that they were American citizens. But although they were playing a sport that was unequivocally American, their chosen team names explicitly championed their Mexican heritage—*Gallos* (Roosters) and *Gallinas* (Hens).

Pictured here is one of the many headlines in northwestern Indiana newspapers reporting on the voluntary and coerced repatriation of both Mexican nationals and Latin Americans to Mexico. Many were native born Americans of Mexican descent.

1940–1949: War Relief, Military Service, and the Arrival of Puerto Ricans

Despite the large wave of deportations during the Great Depression, emigration from Latin American countries and the western United States led to significant growth in Indiana's Latino community during and after World War II. Ten years after thousands of Mexicans were expelled from Indiana, they were being recruited to fill in labor shortages during World War II. In 1942 a binational agreement was reached—the same year a guest agricultural labor program called the Bracero Program started.

Recruitment of foreign, in particular Mexican, agricultural labor in the name of war relief was not a novel concept. This same program was enacted during World War I and was the impetus for growth of the Mexican community in the late 1910s. In the 1940s the program was modified from its predecessor to include greater protections for the guest workers, including provisions that employers guarantee "adequate housing, health and sanitary facilities." However, abuses still occurred.[9] Father John F. Godfrey, who ran Ascension Parish in Chesterfield, Missouri, explained that the actual treatment of the guest workers included substandard housing, which he described as "worse than that required for prisoners of war under the Geneva Convention," as well as brutal working conditions. One newspaper report from September 1954 stated, "Father Godfrey described the collapse of a 16-year-old Mexican boy near Chesterfield after he had worked 16 hours a day, seven days a week, for six weeks."[10]

Migrant workers in tomato field in Grant County, Indiana, 1966

In Indiana *braceros* came to help plant produce such as cucumbers, tomatoes, and other items. They also contributed to the canning and labeling of these products. Mexican workers continued to be represented in these jobs long after the end of the Bracero Program.[11]

Indiana native Claude R. Wickard of Carroll County served as the U.S. Secretary of Agriculture in the Franklin D. Roosevelt Administration, during which time he negotiated with the Mexican government to establish the parameters of the U.S. program. While there were existing migratory and seasonal farmworkers of Mexican descent already working in the United States, this was an expedited call for more. Terms and conditions for employers were to provide housing and sanitary facilities and standard rates of pay. Most of the workers would be recruited to work in the agricultural fields and canneries of the American Southwest and West. Later they would be recruited to work in other war relief employment fields, such as on the railroads. By the first quarter of 1943, there would be approximately 40,000 Mexicans working on farms in the American Southwest.[12] In 1944 the H. J. Heinz Company leased part of a three-hundred-acre farm in Argos, Marshall County, Indiana, to plant and harvest cucumbers for the wartime production of pickles for American sailors. The Heinz company planned to recruit about two hundred Mexican *braceros* to work in the fields.[13]

While recruited Mexican labor would serve as war relief, a cohort of first-generation Mexican Americans would serve their country with distinction as part of the military. Even before the U.S. formally joined the war in 1941, Latinos had already been serving in the U.S. military. Recent estimates show that roughly 500,000 Mexican Americans served during World War II, a reflection of the

deep roots many Latinos had in the United States by this time.[14] Among them was Frederick "Fred" Maravilla, who, with his typing skills, was drafted into the U.S. army and trained for a communications role as a teletype operator for the Army Air Force. But as the enemy forces abandoned their airfields and retreated north, they also destroyed their telephone lines, leaving Maravilla instead with a clerk job while stationed in Foggia, Italy. There he served with the 721st Squadron of the 450th Bombardment Group, part of the Fifteenth Air Force. He was honorably discharged in September 1945 with the rank of corporal.[15]

Back in Indiana, Gloria Guerrero (later Fraire), a noted local star athlete with the all-girls baseball team *Las Gallinas* (formally known as Our Lady Victory Sodality), would serve with the Women's Army Corps (WAC). In 1944 the Lake County Drum and Bugle Corps gave her a farewell party before her transfer to Washington, DC.[16]

Not all Hoosier Latino servicemen and servicewomen came from Lake County. Mr. and Mrs. Cipriano Velásquez of Fairmount in Grant County were informed in late December 1944 that their son, Albert, a Fairmount High School graduate, was reported missing in France. The next spring, the War Department reported that Albert was a prisoner of war in Germany. He would survive his imprisonment and return to his parents, wife Carmen, and their young child. Albert and his growing family would remain in Grant County.

After World War II recruited labor drove a demographic shift that created a diversified Latino community in the Midwest. The next wave of recruited labor came from the U.S. territory of Puerto Rico. A group of five hundred Puerto Ricans arrived in 1948 to help ease the ongoing labor shortage and high turnover rate in local steel mills. They were recruited directly for Carnegie–Illinois Steel, a subsidiary of the U.S. Steel Corporation in Gary. Steel companies of the area worked with labor agencies for recruitment. One in particular was the Samuel J. Friedman Farm Labor Agency, which had its headquarters in San Juan, Puerto Rico. In 1947 this labor agency recruited and brought up several hundred Puerto Ricans to work for the National Tube Company, a subsidiary of U.S. Steel in Lorrain, Ohio. This successful trial immediately prompted recruitment to Gary the following year.[17] Through these efforts, a Puerto Rican community in Northwest Indiana appeared seemingly overnight. As citizens of the United States, they were not required to leave at the end of their contracts. This fact, coupled with the stable and favorable wages of area industry, helped to foster and grow diversity in Indiana's Latino population.

Albert Velásquez with his wife and parents, ca. 1940s. Albert, from Grant County, was drafted into the U.S. Army and later captured in France and sent to a German POW camp.

Gloria Guerrero, from Indiana Harbor, enlisted in the Women's Army Corps during World War II.

1950–1969: Succeeding Generations, *Latin Times,* and Progress

During the 1950s a new generation of Latinos, born and raised in the state, matured into young adults, started their own families, and became community leaders. As in World War II, Hoosier Latinos continued to serve their country in the military and at home. Edward Medina, a second-generation Mexican American who was born in Indiana Harbor, was stationed in West Berlin, Germany, with the U.S. Army during the Korean War. Like Fred Maravilla, he was taught to type at Our Lady of Guadalupe church and later became a clerk for the army. While stationed in Germany, Edward also learned photography, which would become more than a hobby in his later years.[18]

After World War II many first-generation Latinos would struggle with a lack of political pull within their hometown communities, but eventually Hoosier Latinos would find their voice. By the late 1950s they had organized several local chapters of the League of United Latin American Citizens (LULAC) in East Chicago and Gary.[19]

Hoosier Latinos also brought back their community-sourced newspaper, calling it the *Latin Times*. While mainstream news publications were informative, they lacked the voice of the Latinos' growing demographic. The sons of Francisco and Consuelo Figueroa, the publishers of the original Latino newspaper, *El Amigo del Hogar,* resurrected the paper with a Latino community focus similar to that of decades before. One significant difference between the two publications was that the *Latin Times* was primarily in English, with only select columns in Spanish. This was a reflection of the changing cultural duality of the community.

The *Latin Times* was more than an alternative local news source. It served as a source of community empowerment and evidence of belonging in the United States. With their confidence rising, Latinos also began running for local political positions, seeking representation for their community. The sixth district in East Chicago was primarily Mexican, Puerto Rican, and African American. Latinos of this community competed for positions several times before success finally came in 1955 with Joseph Maravilla winning the seat of trustee on the East Chicago School Board. In 1956 he served as president of the East Chicago Board of Education.

The 1960s brought progress across the state for the Latino population, spanning politics, social justice, and education reform. Political progress arrived in 1961 with the election of Jesse Gómez to the East Chicago City Council. While Jesse was born in Indiana Harbor, he had not spent his childhood there. Jesse and his family had been some of the Mexican and native-born U.S. citizens that were expelled from the United States in the 1930s. His family had repatriated to the Mexican state of Zacatecas, but Jesse eventually returned to Indiana Harbor.[20]

Nationally there would be significant legislation aimed at addressing systemic issues affecting Latinos in the United States. President Lyndon B. Johnson made an official call in his 1964 State of the Union Address for a "War on Poverty." Also, this same year the decades-long Bracero Program would end. However, this was not the end of migrant farmworkers traveling to plant and harvest crops in Indiana, just the end of federal funding used to recruit Mexican laborers on a large scale.

Johnson's War on Poverty came through in four pieces of legislation. One in particular, called the Economic Opportunity Act of 1964, established the Economic Opportunity Office funded by federal Title III-B grants. In Indiana in 1965 these federal funds helped incorporate regional nonprofits to form one statewide organization aimed toward the needs of migrant farmworkers, called Associated Migrant Opportunity Services, or AMOS. AMOS was formed by the Council of Indiana Churches and the Catholic Archdioceses in Indianapolis, Gary, Lafayette, and in Fort Wayne–South Bend.[21] Information centers were dotted around the state in counties in the northwestern, north central, central, and southern areas of Indiana. Prior to the formation of AMOS, volunteers in local churches partnered with the faith-based national organization called Migrant Ministry that led migrant outreach. Thus, Indiana was an example of the changing national perspective toward migrant workers, which was shifting from charity to advocacy.

Carmen Velásquez experienced this shift in perspective. Initially, she worked independently in Marion, Grant County, with the support of the local Catholic church, addressing the material and spiritual needs of local migrant farmers. Her father-in-law, Cipriano Velásquez, representing one of the few Latino families in the area, owned and operated his own farm in Grant County. Already a fixture in the community, Carmen helped establish the AMOS–East sub-office in Marion, Indiana, under Director Benito López.[22]

To the east of Indianapolis, in Henry County, Raúl and Rogelia Piñon worked for Brooks Foods, before and after settling in Indiana. Brooks Foods was first established as Mount Summit Products in 1925 and was renamed Brooks Foods in 1956. The company grew seasonal crops and operated a canning facility until it closed in 1997. Based on the Piñons' 2016 oral history interview, they were the first Latinos to permanently settle in this area in the winter of 1962, initially residing in Pumpkintown, an unincorporated area just outside of Mount Summit. Migrant farmworker organizations call this "settling out," when migrant farmworkers leave the migratory stream and settle in an area to obtain steady, year-round work. More important, migratory families "settle out" so their children can receive an education that normally would be disrupted by travel for planting

AMOS worker inspects migrant camp in Delaware County, 1960s

Fred Maravilla (middle) is pictured with his brother Joe (left) and his father Ignacio (right) at Fred's Master of Arts Commencement from the University of Chicago in June 1955. With his degrees, Fred became a teacher and college instructor.

and picking seasons.[23] The Piñon family would later settle in Mount Summit proper. Rogelia continued to work for Brooks Foods for a short time. Raúl continued to work in the agricultural industry at a plant nursery into his late eighties.

As Latinos began to find permanent places to work and live as far back as the 1940s, there were some who did not fully welcome them. During the mid-1940s, for example, in Irvington, an eastside Indianapolis neighborhood, a small group objected to plans to house some railroad workers in a

home there.[24] Despite this type of bias, Latino farmworkers and those in other fields of work across the state continued their contributions, and new members of the community continued to arrive.

In 1965 the United States entered the Vietnam War. Now the Latino struggle would be on domestic and international fronts. While another generation of Hoosier Latino servicemen and women fought on behalf of the United States, César Chávez, the head of the AFL–CIO (American Federation of Labor–Congress of Industrial Organizations)

Children of migrant workers in dwelling within migrant camp in Grant County, 1966

United Farm Workers Organizing Committee, led what is remembered as the California Grape Strike and National Boycott, finally winning concessions from the growers in 1970.[25]

In addition to facing discrimination in labor, Latinos also struggled during these years to address disparities in the educational system. Senator Ralph Yarborough of Texas introduced national legislation in 1967 focusing on the needs of LESA (Limited English-Speaking Ability) students. Title VII of the Civil Rights Act was subsequently amended with the Bilingual Education Act in 1968.[26] This same year, Hispanic Heritage Week was introduced in recognition of a growing population.

This era of tumultuous growth began with the intense struggle of the Great Depression, which led to federal and local deportation policies that drastically reduced the Latino population in Indiana. But the remainder of the period showcased the Latinos' resiliency and commitment to their Hoosier home as the population bounced back quickly, aided by the influx of guest workers that began arriving in the 1940s under the Bracero Program. The growing Hoosier Latino population provided many young men and women for service in the armed conflicts of the times. They served in Europe, Japan, Korea, and Vietnam. As this era ended, Latinos were just beginning to exert their voices on the Hoosier political landscape as the Chicano

Civil Rights Movement, which had begun in the American Southwest, began exerting its presence in the state. At the same time, the early *barrios*, or Spanish-speaking neighborhoods, in Indiana Harbor and Indianapolis that had grown substantially over the decades were being dispersed by local governments.

1920s–1969: Lost *Barrios* of Indiana Harbor and Indianapolis

Barrio is not a term you would associate with the Midwest, much less Indiana. *Barrio* is often associated with an urban, non-Midwest, close-knit community where the primary language is Spanish. A *barrio* forms more by circumstance than chance, and these circumstances carve out a space that serves as a foundation for the vibrant Latino community that is created. The following is an examination of two *barrios* in Indiana Harbor in East Chicago and India-

napolis, during the first half of the twentieth century until their erasure at the end of the 1960s.

The first acknowledgment of the Indiana Harbor *barrio* came in newsprint; the *Hammond Times* on July 10, 1923, labeled this area "little Mexico." This nickname would be used continuously to describe Indiana Harbor throughout the decades. As this lakefront area grew, so did the approximately half-mile square known as Block and Pennsy. This neighborhood served as a readily available source of low-paid Mexican labor from the late 1910s through the 1920s.[27]

The 1920s would see an increase in the Mexican population. Demographically, this would be a change from *solos* to families and middle-class Mexicans, mostly from west central Mexico. Changes in demographics were attributed to post-Mexican Revolution skirmishes fueled by the Cristero War. Mutual Aid and social/cultural societies emerged in

The Gallinas *Women's Baseball Team, Indiana Harbor, 1938. Fred Maravilla (far right, back row) was the team manager that year.*

FREDERICK RUIZ MARAVILLA, INDIANA HISTORICAL SOCIETY

The Gallos *Men's Baseball Team, Indiana Harbor, 1939*

Indiana Harbor to meet the needs of this growing community. The overall exponential population growth in this decade would surpass the pace of building new residential dwellings. By 1930 there were 934 Mexican families in Indiana Harbor and only 13 of those families were property owners.[28]

By the late 1950s approximately 1,800 individuals called Block and Pennsy home. The population was primarily Black and Latino, and the neighborhood was known for stable, low rents. A second generation of individuals was aging in place in crowded homes with substandard infrastructure and in tenements dating back to the founding of Indiana Harbor. A rent control program sustained the residents until 1951 when the city council terminated the program for the entire city.[29] Lack of appropriate housing stock and the inability to rent or buy in certain areas of the city due to an intentional pattern of segregation caused families to seek housing in neighboring cities. Additionally, as the *Hammond Times* reported in 1951, Inland Steel was planning to construct four new open-hearth furnaces in addition to the thirty-six already in operation. Thousands more workers would be needed in 1952. The necessity for labor would be as acute as it was in the late 1910s and 1920s. Suddenly there was an urgency to improve living conditions for the Block and Pennsy neighborhood in Indiana Harbor.

The federal Housing Act of 1954 would set into motion a series of urban renewal plans for Indiana Harbor, East Chicago, Hammond, and Gary. Urban Renewal Project No. 1, for Indiana Harbor, was the first of several projects to be implemented in the area. The *Latin Times*, serving as the voice of East Chicago Latinos, began reporting on the development of the urban renewal project starting in 1957. Initially, the paper's editorial pieces were in favor of this plan, seeing it as a way to increase the quality of life

Photo of Mi Ranchito *restaurant at 3439 Pennsylvania Avenue in the Indiana Harbor* barrio, ca. 1963–71

for Indiana Harbor Latinos. The plan noted opportunities for financial assistance and residential rehabilitation for improving existing living conditions. Urban Renewal Project No. 1 would be executed by the East Chicago Redevelopment Corporation, a subsidiary of the Purdue–Calumet Redevelopment Foundation. Formed in 1954, the foundation's goal was to facilitate "access to land areas needed for the broad solution of the house, population and racial problems."[30]

Initial steps toward improving city conditions started in 1958 with proposed new zoning laws by the East Chicago City Council. After the zoning was accepted, Urban Renewal Project No. 1 was approved in 1959. The approval cited the plan as a benefit to the city and public utility. The impetus for the city council to propose this ordinance was that the "people are too deeply congested" and "we are rearranging use of land to accommodate more families and at the same time provide more and better facilities." The zoning ordinance and this plan would give individuals the opportunity to repair properties, and the Purdue–Calumet foundation would provide financial and architectural assistance. City Council President John Grdinich stated that when the project was complete, more people living in that area would be living in better conditions. The first order of the plan

was for slum removal and the building of low-income and medium-income homes and units. The executive secretary of the East Chicago Redevelopment Commission, Thomas S. Bunsa, confidently stated, "Before anyone has to move, 300 new houses will be constructed." Not all residents were convinced of this ordinance or of the urban renewal plan. Willie Collier of 3600 Block Avenue requested that a provision of the outline be put on record. Elizabeth Jackson of the 3800 block of Pennsylvania Avenue objected to having her house leveled for a playground. Mrs. C. T. Sanders, also of this block, complained that properties were in disrepair and were unable to be updated due to the immigrants attracted to the Block and Pennsy Area.[31] These were the final arguments from residents in debates regarding the plan.

In 1960, East Chicago, as many urban cities, was experiencing a boom of infrastructure development with the groundbreaking for the Cline Avenue Expressway, an overpass for U.S. Route 20. Cline Avenue was on the northern border of Block and Pennsy. The purpose for the overpass was to alleviate heavy industrial traffic in a residential area; the traffic was destined for the Inland Steel Company.

The *Latin Times* editors initially thought favorably of the project and the new zoning, but lack of transparency and resident involvement quickly changed this positive

Jesus Arredondo (second from left) with other bakers inside P. H. Bakery's kitchen. P. H. Bakery, owned by Plácido Hernández, was located at 3805 Pulaski Street in Indiana Harbor.

outlook. The paper's critique of the project was heightened the same year as the opening of the Saint Lawrence Seaway, which connected the Great Lakes to the Atlantic Ocean for the purpose of increasing commercial vessel traffic for area industries. Overnight the Lake Michigan lakefront neighborhood of Block and Pennsy and the land it inhabited appeared exponentially valuable, while property owners were given nominal buyouts to accommodate the new highway.

A new mayoral administration in 1964 noted that Urban Renewal Project No. 1 had built no residential buildings. Instead it parceled away the Block and Pennsy neighborhood by demolition, forcing those who were displaced to live in temporary mobile homes. Because of this, residents of the neighborhood were anxious and distrustful of the local government. The lack of residential building was attributed to land negotiation with the B&O (Baltimore and Ohio) Railroad, which owned land adjacent to the southern border of Block and Pennsy.

Finally, that same year, ground was broken for the first residential project—Cal–View Apartments. These apartments would provide housing for 255 families, with rents ranging from $94 to $139 per month. They would be located on Guthrie Street in clusters between Elm and Lincoln Streets. Positive and visible momentum of the project eased some of the residents' tensions. However, this was short-lived. In 1965 federal funding for the renewal project was significantly reduced, citing the lack of progress.[32] The Cal–View Apartments, totaling fifteen residential structures, would not be completed until 1967.

The years 1966 through 1968 were turbulent with public accusations and admittance of kickbacks and unethical dealings by two mayoral administrations. The Purdue–Calumet Development Foundation reported in 1968 that a total of 1,528 individuals had been displaced since the start of the urban renewal program but that only 1,175 had been successfully relocated. Less than two-thirds of the residents of Block and Pennsy at the start of the project in 1960 remained in the neighborhood. This report and the accusations of impropriety left Urban Renewal Project No.1 marred by its failure to rehabilitate residences and retain Indiana Harbor residents.

City officials of East Chicago in 1969 would publicly seek to end the city's contract with the Purdue–Calumet Development Foundation. Residential redevelopment of Indiana Harbor and East Chicago, however, would continue.[33]

Before Indiana Harbor was christened "little Mexico," the city of Indianapolis would boast in a 1916 *Indianapolis News* article that there were one hundred Mexicans living in Indianapolis. The article mentioned that this small community was composed mostly of university students and a few businessmen, who were displaced by the Mexican Revolution. Where these *Mexicanos* lived is uncertain. It is likely they were interspersed in different neighborhoods.[34]

By the 1940s growth of the city's Latino community would be evident. Much like other ethnic groups, they were attracted to Indianapolis by well-paid jobs in factories and on the railroad. Their *barrio* existed within the following borders: East North Street to the north, Market Street to the south, Davidson Street to the west, and North Pine Street to the east. Many of the families who lived in the community were born in Mexico and spent time in the western United States before coming to Indianapolis to

MÉNDEZ FAMILY

Francisca Méndez sits in her yard with three children during the early 1930s. She lived with her husband and children at 428 North Pine Street, Indianapolis.

Three Quintana brothers stand outside of their home on Davidson Street in Indianapolis during the early 1950s. Hogan and Mayflower storage buildings and a Jungclaus–Campbell smokestack are visible in the background.

work. A few families came from Mercedes, Hidalgo County, Texas. The local Catholic church, Saint Mary, on the corner of New Jersey and Vermont Streets, offered worship services in Spanish. The adjacent Marian Center provided limited educational services to the growing Latino community.

A small enclave of Mexicans and Texan Mexicans settled on the east side of downtown Indianapolis. A collection of transcripts from 1990 lists by name some of the families who settled in this area. Jesús "Jesse" Quintana, distinctively called this area of downtown "*El Barrio*" in an oral history interview.[35] Two of the earliest members of this close-knit community were Francisca and Gabino Méndez of west central Mexico. Prior to settling in Indianapolis between 1927–30, they had spent their early years in the

United States in western Kansas. The Méndezes hosted as boarders in their rental home on East Ohio Street Cristóbal and Guadalupe García. Later the Méndezes would call 428 Pine Street home. Francisca would become a strong advocate for assimilation, viewing it as a necessity for survival and success. Other noted individuals and families in the Indianapolis *barrio* were Noé Morales, José Riojas, Ernesto Cervantes, Paulina Zamora, and Manuel and Adel Segovia.[36]

The railroad industry brought Jesse Quintana and Feliciano Espinoza to Indianapolis. There were multiple railroad companies in town that employed a large number of Mexican Americans and Mexicans. Labor recruiters in the 1920s and 1930s were noted as going to Kansas City and Saint Louis to recruit Mexican section hands working in railroad labor gangs.[37]

Feliciano "Felix" Espinoza bags groceries at his store, El Nopal Market, located at 801 East North Street, Indianapolis, during the 1960s.

As the community grew, so did their needs for social outlets to celebrate and preserve their culture. In 1958 the *Indianapolis Star* reported on the election of officers for the Social Mexicano Club at Christamore House, a historic settlement house in the westside Haughville neighborhood. Officers sworn in were a local attorney, a doctor, and an eastside *barrio* resident, Feliciano Espinoza.[38]

By the mid-1960s, one of the city's earliest Mexican-owned grocery stores, *El Nopal* Market, operated in the neighborhood at 810 East North Street. Its owners were Feliciano "Felix" and María Espinoza. The Mexican market occupied the first floor as a storefront in the Espinoza family home. Their reach expanded outside of Indianapolis when they traveled on the weekends to the surrounding farmland of central Indiana. The Espinozas sold musical records, produce, tortillas, and other goods to seasonal and migrant farmworkers.

Just like the residents of the Block and Pennsy neighborhood of Indiana Harbor, Indianapolis's *barrio* residents would be affected by urban revitalization, specifically with the development of interstates I-65 and I-70. The Espinozas' neighborhood was parceled away by eminent domain buyouts and demolition. Their family's *El Nopal* Market was one of the last holdouts at the end of the 1960s. After falling victim to eminent domain, the grocery briefly moved into the City Market, but it ceased operation in the early 1970s.

Although the residents were displaced, traces of this eastside downtown Latino community would remain. Feliciano Espinoza, Tulio Guldner, and other community members founded a social organization catering to the needs of the community. In 1971, just blocks away from the *barrio* at 617 East North Street, the Hispano-American Multi-Service Center was established. It would be commonly known as *El Centro* or the Hispanic Center.

History in Their Own Words: Stories from the Era of Tumultuous Growth

Fred Maravilla

Fred Maravilla came to Indiana Harbor as a small child, graduated from an East Chicago high school, and served in the U.S. military during World War II. Afterward, he returned to his wife and daughter in Indiana, used the GI Bill to go to college, and became a high school teacher and a college instructor. In the following interview excerpts he discusses his experiences during the Great Depression and World War II.

Date of Interview: September 24, 2016 | Age at time of interview: 98 years

Memories of Mexican Repatriation during the Great Depression

FM: *So, in the 1930 census there were about 5,000 Mexicans in East Chicago. Most of them lived in Indiana Harbor, in a small part of Indiana Harbor—'bout half a mile square. Actually, about a mile in two streets—from one end of the street to the other, Block and Pennsy [Pennsylvania], Deodar Street, Elm—well within a very small area. There were about 5,000 Mexicans in Indiana Harbor and about 1,000 of them were actually deported, sent back to Mexico. There was one friend of ours—one friend of mine, his name was Cipriano Hernández. His family—the whole family was going to go. They had three or four children, father and mother—they were all packed and*

Fred Maravilla was drafted into the U.S. Army during World War II. He served in the Mediterranean Theatre as part of the 450th Bombardment Group in Italy. He is pictured here in 1944.

FREDERICK RUIZ MARAVILLA, INDIANA HISTORICAL SOCIETY

on the train, ready to go, and the father said: "Hey—where is Cipriano? Cipriano is missing!" And they looked all through the train and there was no Cipriano. Cipriano (laughs) had taken off and gone over to the Lake Michigan.[39]

NML: [Laughs] He was hiding in the lake?

FM: *He ran away. [Laughs] He didn't want to go to Mexico, so the family had to get off the train and not leave—which ended up being a good thing because in a year or two, the mills started. Nineteen thirty-three as a matter of fact, the mill, Inland Steel, Youngstown Sheet and Tube—started rehiring and they picked up, they started to work again, but that family would have gone to Mexico if Cipriano hadn't run away. [Both laugh] And the father and mother weren't happy at first. [Laughs] I think they gave him a good beating, but after a while they said they were glad that he did what he did. But it was sad to see all those people leave.*

NML: Where were the trains leaving from? Where was the train depot?

FM: *The train depot? There was a train depot in Indiana Harbor on Guthrie Street [and Michigan Avenue] that they would embark in. There was a newspaper, the* Latin Times *that printed pictures of the large crowd saying goodbye to the people who were going back to Mexico. And many of them went back to Mexico and they went from bad to worse because—Mexico was a poor country and didn't have what the United States had. They had just gotten over that—the [Mexican] Revolution of 1910 and were just rebuilding. The revolution was a very sad thing for Mexico. They lost about 10 percent of the population to the revolution. . . .*

And my father wanted us to go. He says, "I will stay here until the work starts up and I will go bring you back."

But my mother was adamant. She said, "I am not going back to Mexico. My father has four children that he has to take care of. . . . All he has is a little plot of land, and if I go with my two children it will just be another big burden on him."

So we stayed then. Like I said, my mother pulled us through—and I am glad, otherwise we may—if we would have gone, we may not have come back.

But many people, I know one family, the López family. The mother went back with a one-year-old boy and a daughter and three other sons. And the one-year-old died within a year that they got there, and the mother soon after that passed away also. Conditions in Mexico were much different than here—(sigh) the López family."

NML: How did you know that they had passed away? Were you writing letters to them?

Opposite: Fred Maravilla (front, far left) with other servicemen of the 721st headquarter staff in Italy, 1944

FM: *They were from the same town that we were [from], and the husband stayed [in Indiana Harbor], Mariano, who eventually became my compadre. And they were very close friends from back home, back from Guarachita or Villamar, very, very dear close friends. They were compadres actually with my parents, compadres. And the older one, they all came back except the little boy [and the mother] who died. But eventually Mariano, the father, sent for them. He kept them there for a while because the schools in Mexico were—if you attended school you got a good education. And Henry López when he came back, he was the same age as my brother. He [Henry] came back, he was very much ahead in mathematics compared to the students here [Indiana Harbor] and in world history, he acquired a good education in Mexico. He served—Indiana and two of his brothers served in the war [World War II]. But it was very sad [the overall effects of World War II].*

One thing though, they couldn't take everything they had with them. So people who stayed back got the leftovers that they couldn't take with them. I acquired some silk shirts—collarless, because the silk shirts at the time had a celluloid collar. . . . I would go to high school (laughs) with a silk shirt. . . . (laughs) And bib overalls (laughs). . . . But it was a sad period [to live in].

Service in World War II

FM: *I got married in 1942 and in July, July the 4th of 1942, and went on the honeymoon to New York City and saw the* Normandie, *the ship that had been—I think that it—our own dock workers are the ones who torched it, and it didn't sink but it was over on its side.[40] The bright lights were no longer bright because we were in the—had already declared war. But we spent a couple of weeks in New York City and then came back home. And I went to work, and the day after I went to work I had to go to the hospital because I had an appendicitis attack. And while I was in the hospital—this was in July. I got my notice that I was eligible for the draft and ended up going into the service as a draftee. . . .*

I was in Galveston, Texas, at the time, and I got a ride on the B-17 up to Nebraska—Lincoln, Nebraska. And took a train to Chicago and then down by bus to Indiana Harbor. The Red Cross had arranged for me to get a furlough because of the birth of my daughter. And after my furlough was over, I was [shipped] to Alamogordo in New Mexico where I joined the 450th at the Bomb Group, that's where it materialized. And the early part of December we embarked from Virginia, we were scheduled to go to North Africa but our orders were changed. We—in December of '43, we spent the night in Bizerte [Tunisia], North Africa and the following day landed in Naples, Foggia.[41] The battle line was only five or six miles north of Naples at the time. You could hear the volleys of artillery and you could even see the flashes of the explosions. The Germans had a very talented field marshal. He was holding the line. The line at the time was Naples–Foggia, straight across the African—the Italian Peninsula, but he had already fortified another line farther north, the Rome–Arno line, and he kept doing that all through the war. We never were able to conquer all of Italy.[42]

NML: Who was he? The Germans? Hitler? Just so that our readers would know when you represent "he." You said he. . . ?

FM: *The German field marshal.[43]*

NML: Ok, got it.

FM: *Yes, the German field marshal was a very good strategist and he kept forming these lines and we would, you know, overtake him on one, but he had already had his defenses ready, and we never were able, we were going to supposedly penetrate there and going into Germany. We never accomplished that purpose. Before [the] 450th acquired four campaigns in Italy, they ended up with ten, and four of them were Italian, the Italian campaigns.[44] But in any case, we left the day after we landed by truck convoy down to Manduria, Italy. Which was in the heel part of the peninsula, about twenty-five miles from Taranto, the naval base.[45] And we took over an old Italian airfield, reinforced the runways with steel planking, and started flying missions in January of 1944. We—I was very fortunate because I had picked up, we were scheduled to go to Africa—French possession—and on the way there—it took us about twenty-three days to cross the ocean. I picked [up] a little bit of French from a French grammar book thinking that we would be stationed in Tunisia or [within the] French possession.[46] But as I said, we went to Italy instead.*

But Italian is so much like Spanish that I picked up Italian very quickly and, among other things, I became the translator for the soldiers, the Italian soldiers who had been let go after the Italian army capitulated. They were set free, and we used them as laborers to do the work around the camp, do the clean-up and work in the kitchen and do all the menial labors that the soldiers would have had to do. So [the airmen] were able to devote all of their time to the war effort. And since the Germans had carted away anything of value as they retreated, there were no telephone wires for telephone lines. So, my job as a teletype operator went out the window [laughs], and I became a clerk typist.

And then my commanding officer [told me], "Maravilla, you are pretty good with words. I want you to compose a letter of regrets to send to the families. We—are going to have casualties."

So that was one of my jobs. I started off composing a separate letter for each casualty we had, but eventually we had so many casualties that we ended up using a form letter, same thing over and over again, just filling the blanks. There were 5,000 men who served in the 450th; 1,005 were killed or missing in action. We sustained a lot of casualties because of the German fighter planes attacking the formation, until the latter part of June of 1944 when the Tuskegee Airmen took over. And they came over and they had a brand-new plane that was very well armed and had protection for the pilot and—it was the fastest plane available at the time.[47] *And the Tuskegee Airmen were so [deft], were so well trained that we never lost a plane after that to fighter action. We lost many planes because of the target; the flak was so heavy. As I say we lost out of 5,000 men who served in the 450th, we lost 1,005, killed or missing in action.*

NML: Who were [the] 450th Bomb Group? Were they like Tuskegee Airmen, were they Latino, were they just mixed?

FM: *No, they were few Latinos in the group. Very few.*

NML: Did you join up with other men from Indiana Harbor? Other Latino men?

FM: *No. I met only one [non-Latino] person from Indiana Harbor and that was toward the end of the war. He graduated in 1944 from Washington High School. . . . That's where I went to high school. He was a boy of Jewish extraction. I can't think of his name now. [His name was Joseph Seigal, graduated 1942]. But he was the only one that I met from Indiana Harbor. It was another one that whenever we went to visit a town, we would go to a place where the GIs would sign in. And there was another student from Washington High School who signed in before I did, and I never was able to get, but—never able to meet anyone else from Indiana Harbor.*

Well, the war ended, and our outfit was scheduled to go to the Pacific—we had already reconquered some of the islands close to Japan, and the B-17s and B-24s were scheduled to go there and bomb Japan.[48] *But I never—my outfit didn't have to go. But anyhow—at the end of the hostilities in Europe, the government put up a program—they knew they had to demobilize, they couldn't use all of the personnel. So, they used a program and gave a certain number of points—for the age of the military personnel, so many points for his age, so many points if he was married, so many points if he had dependents, so many points for the number of months he had served in the armed forces, and so many points that he had served overseas. And I happened to fall into the category that had enough points to demobilize. So, I was stretched out of my outfit for the mobilization process.*

My commanding officers said, "Fred, if you stay with us, you all can go up in rank the minute we go to the Pacific."

I said, "No thank you, sir [laughs], but I am going home [laughs]."

Edward Medina

Edward Medina was born into the Mexican community of Northwest Indiana and served in the U.S. Army. He worked in the steel industry and as a photographer. In the following interview excerpts he discusses the Great Depression, his army service in Germany, and his work as a photographer.

Date of interview: September 1, 2016 | Age at time of interview: 86 years

Weathering the Great Depression

NML: So, as you moved, did your apartments get bigger, or why did you move so much?

EM: *I don't know. Maybe it was bigger, better accommodations. I know that when we lived on Pulaski Street, [it] was a four-room, little apartment, two bedrooms, a living room, and a kitchen. There was a pantry and a washroom. My father, mother, my older sister Grace and I lived there with my mother's parents, José and María Picón Reyes. And I guess it was done for economy purposes because times were hard. Don't forget, we are talking the '30s. Depression is in there, things were not moving too good, very slow. I remember my dad would go to the mill every morning, and then the foremen would come out and they would pick up certain workers. So, if a man got a job one or two or three days a week, he was doing good and for the conditions, it was tough. I remember we used to—one time I went with my father, because we went to, I forget the name of the organization, but they used to provide food for some of the people.*[49] *Over in the mill they would give tickets or something and then they would go to pick up this—everything was no brand names or anything like that. . . . All were generic, everything was black and white, cans had a white label with black lettering, big black lettering. Cereals and everything else were white cardboard box with letters crossed, black letters in cereal or whatever.*

NML: And so, did your dad get work often during the Depression?

EM: *Yes, and the foremen would, I think they would pick the ones that some of them were better workers. So my dad was fortunate, [my] grandfather was also, that they would get picked. . . .*

NML: So, I also know that in the 1930s, and I don't know if you remember, there was something called the repatriation trains, where you know, during the Depression a lot of Mexican individuals or families went back to Mexico, either voluntarily or involuntarily. . . . Do you remember anything about that or [have you] heard anything about that?

EM: *Well no, because look, I was born October 1929. In about thirty days after that, the stock market falls. In other words, it just took me thirty days to crash this thing.*

NML: Yeah, when you were born. (Laughs)

EM: *So, the stock market fell, and it was in November? . . . Yeah, because I was born in October and in November it crashed. So, I am already in the '30s, things are tough; things are very, very bad. That's when the repatriation starts. Fortunately, I guess that my father was working, my grandfather was working, we did not, we were not a burden to anybody, we were still being able to maintain our own selves and I guess they were kind of picking most of the people that were not working, were not able to provide for themselves and they were going to become a burden to the state. So, they had to take those people or anybody who was willing to go.*

NML: Yeah, so I know that it was, I've read a lot on that of a lot of people who left and you know, some people were even U.S. citizens.

EM: *My cousins left. They went back to Monterrey, the Ríos family, my father's sister. . . . Yeah, No, he stood here. This was my father's sister, Carmen Reyes [Ríos], Carmen Medina Reyes [Ríos]. She went back with her family, in fact. And their sons became tourist guides in Mexico because they spoke English and Spanish and people would come down there: "Hey I can show you this," and they knew how to communicate with them in English.*[50]

Joining the Army

EM: *Yeah, during the time that I was there, Uncle Sam decided to invite me to go play soldier with him. They had what they would call draft. So, I had to go for active service for two years and then serve four years as inactive. . . . So, for the first two years, Uncle Sam took me off to Kansas and trained me over there on all kind of different infantry weapons, and then he put me on the ship in January and took me over to the north Atlantic, and the ship went up and down and up and down. And I got seasick when I got there, and he took me to the northern part of Germany to live [dock] in a town called Bremerhaven. . . .*[51] *And*

then they put me on a train, and the train came straight down Germany and this is one of the little short trains at the—they are not long cars like we have railroad cars, but shorter cars. And the rails have the joints, okay? . . . And each time you get one of these joints you got a bump. . . . So, being in a regular long car, when the train is going, it is going "ca lick a lick . . . ca lick a lick" where the wheels are going over the joints. When you have a shorter railroad car, the wheels are going to hit that joint more often. So, instead of going "ba dump a dump . . . ba dump a dump" [mimicking noise of car], then it is going "ba dump a dump ba dump a dump" [at a quicker pace] this way. After being seasick on the ship, you get into something like that, coming from the northern part of Germany to the French border. . . . Oh, oh! Uncle Sam saved money by not feeding me (laughs). I couldn't eat. . . .

It took us to a little place named Zweibrücken, which means two brooks.[52] *And then from there they got distributed to different places. I got sent to Berlin, where I stood there for a year and a half and I learned enough German to get into trouble, but also enough to get out of it. . . . I learned how to apologize in German.*[53]

NML: Do you still remember a little German?

EM: *Oh, a little (laughs) . . . Guten Tag, Gute Nacht, wie gehts, was machen Sie, ich entschuldige mich, bitte. . . . [Good day! Good night! How's it going? What do you do? I apologize. Sorry.]*

NML: Okay. So you said, so what did you do in Berlin?

EM: *Well, at first in Berlin I was assigned to a heavy weapons company. And the heavy weapons company at that time, they were out in the field, they were shooting with machine guns, training with machine guns. I went there, and all they had me doing was putting the links together because it was like a figure eight link, and you put two rounds in there, you keep attaching and you got a long belt. This belt feeds into the machine that we go, "tat tat tat tat tat tat tat" [mimicking noise of machine]. And the belt had disintegrated into these figure eight links. . . . That's what us new guys were doing. And then we got the chance to fire. I managed to be, to get the top score. . . . I was in the army, and I went in 1952. I came in 195—no, 1951. I came out in 1953. . . .*

NML: So, did you have a job while you were in the army, or you just did training?

EM: *No, then I got assigned to heavy weapons company. And then because of the manner in which you fired the machine gun, it was elevated towards to go, instead of firing on 1,000 yards,* you fire on a target that was 1,000 inches away from you, but it had a pattern; you had to put your bullets into that pattern.

And because I ended up getting top score, the lieutenant was a West Point man, and he says, "Where did you learn to fire so good?"[54]

I said, "Simple, it's like using a typewriter."

He said, "You are a typist, huh?"

I said, "A little bit." I had learned how to type. . . .

Where did I learn how to type? Before I graduated, you know, I was an altar boy. There was a French priest, and he used to tell me, "What did I do?"

"Oh, I do nothing, I don't know, play basketball, play football."

He said, "No, no, you got to do something useful."

I said: "Well, okay, what?"

He says: "You are going to learn how to type."

"Why do I want to learn how to type?"

"Believe me it will be handy for you. You will have made it; you can use it in a lot of different ways. You will learn, you want to learn how to type? I will teach you how to type. You want to learn how to type? I will devote time to teach you. I want you one hour, five days a week; not two hours, not half an hour; not three days, not four days, five days. Five days a week, one hour a week [sic], each day, and in four weeks I will have you typing."

"Okay." A-S-T-S-semi colon-L-K-J-space. I had a heck of a time trying to get that thing going. . . . I learned how to type, and then the bank that helped me up because I was able to type, too.

And when I went in the army and I beat everybody else with the machine gun, the guy said: "So you are a typist, okay." No more heavy weapons company for me. I got upstairs to the headquarters, and I worked at S4, at the supply office.

Photographing the Community

NML: So, did you start becoming a freelance photographer right away, like once you came back from your wedding?

EM: No. There was a newspaper that started up called the Latin Times, and they asked me if I could help them. So I used to be, I used to like to draw cartoons and stuff like that, so I helped them design the head logo for the Times and then they said, "We need pictures and stuff like that."

Edward Medina was drafted into the U.S. Army during the Korean War. He was stationed in West Berlin, Germany, as part of the post-World War II occupation by western Allies. He is shown here in Germany in 1951.

Well okay, I said, "I'll go out." So, I would go out to different events and take pictures there and come back home, develop them. They would pay me for the pictures, just for the material, sort of like a contribution, not pay me a salary or anything like that. And—

NML: Just to get your name in the paper?

EM: *Yeah, kind of, sort of, I saw that I was able to make some pictures because people wanted copies of it.*

NML: So, what kind of pictures did you take for them?

EM: *Just a local.*

NML: So, was the *Latin Times* just for East Chicago residents?

EM: *Just the local.*

NML: Just the local. So, what did they report on?

EM: *Social events, birthdays, maybe other things that are of importance to the community that would happen in that particular place, or informative stuff. I remember one picture I took of a place that burned down in Cudahy.[55] There was a little section called Cudahy. . . . Just out of Indiana Harbor going towards Gary. . . . And there was a Cudahy Packing Company there, and it was close by to that housing section that these people used to have houses there. I remember the house burned down, and I went and took a picture. But the only thing that I was able to take a picture of was a pump because they had this water pump where they used to get their water from. You couldn't pump the water fast enough to throw into the—"*

NML: Kind of like, before the fire hydrant, so this was really old.

EM: *It was nothing but ashes in the back and a blur, with the water pump. I told Gus [Figueroa] to print that, and he says: "This is a nice idea, but what are we going to sell?" We would just tell them the house burned down. Look at that, because that's all they had to fight, they needed regular water [pump] out there and what not. I don't remember if he printed it or not. . . . Yeah, Gus Figueroa was the editor. . . .*

NML: When did it start? Do you remember? Was it always around when you were a kid?

EM: *No, no, because it started when I was there. . . . It's got to be after '54 because I was, you know, I already married. . . . '54, '55, '56, something like that. Yeah, it should be in the archives some place around where it's registered and what not."*

NML: So, Gus Figueroa was the owner of the newspaper?

EM: *Yeah, they were the owners. The Figueroa printers were the owners. . . . On Deodar Street . . . right across the street from my house. . . . A couple doors down was the V. F. Garza place where they used to make cheese and chorizo.*

NML: So, it seems like everybody lived, I think, within a couple of blocks of each other—or all the Latinos did.

EM: *No, that was just my section. But if you go across the tracks all of Block and Pennsy, Watling, Michigan Avenue, the other famous Aragola [Arredondo] family, they used to live on the Michigan Avenue there. No, there was, we were starting to spread out.*

Edward Medina self-portrait

Sandra Valdés

Sandra Valdés is the child of Mexican immigrants who met in Indiana Harbor in the 1920s and became reacquainted in Mexico in the 1940s. They married there and returned to Indiana Harbor together. Born and raised in Indiana Harbor, Sandra has been an education and human resources professional. In this interview excerpt she discusses her mother, María del Refugio Ramírez (later Godínez) and her and her parents' return to Mexico. She reads a letter from her mother to the Mexican *colonia* that was printed in the early Indiana Harbor newspaper, *El Amigo del Hogar*.

Date of Interview: November 14, 2017 | Age at time of interview: 69 years | Interview transcript audited by Nancy M. Germano (2017–18)

Sandra Valdés on Returning to Mexico during the Great Depression

SV: *During that time, well, like I said, in 1928 my mom, my grandmother, my uncle, they returned to Mexico because they heard that the Depression was coming. . . .*[56] *So, they thought, "We better—better leave." So, they did. They left. And my mom—really, what she started doing was, like, cleaning a doctor's office. Yeah. But then those doctors were, like—they had a cancer clinic. So, they taught her how to use all the equipment. . . .*

NML: Okay. So, she became queen in 1926, and then they left two years later. And so, will you read the letter that she wrote in the newspaper because some of it is, kind of, cut off? . . .

SV: *(Sandra reads the* El Amigo del Hogar *article and mother's letter in Spanish.)* [See copy of letter at right.]

NML: And so—so the gist of the—

SV: *So, just giving thanks for—to the—Uh-huh—the community or—uh-huh—and (pauses to review the letter) they will always live in their, like, in their heart, and that maybe they can soon return to their* patria—*to their homeland. . . . Yeah. This is not a good-bye, but a* hasta luego *[See you later].*

Página 6

Para Guadalajara

La Sra. Doña Josefa Cedillo Vda. de Ramírez y su hija la bella señorita Ma. del Refugio Ramírez, Reina de las fiestas Patrias de Indiana Harbor, el año de 1926, salieron para la ciudad de Guadalajara, donde residirán.

A continuación tenemos el gusto de publicar la atenta carta, por medio de la cual se despide de la H. Colonia.

Indiana Harbor, Ind. Oct. 31 de 1928

Sr. Director del Semananario
"HUMO"
Ciudad.

Muy señor nuestro:

Teniendo el gran placer de regresar a la amada Patria, no he querido abandonar este lugar sin antes hacer públicos mis agradecimientos por la forma en que he sido tratada de parte de las H. Sociedades y de la H. Colonia en general, pues en verdad deben todos los compatriotas residentes en este lugar, estar seguros de que siempre vivirán en mi corazón, y que hago votos por que muy pronto puedan regresar al regazo de la amorosa madre.

Este no es un adios, sino un hasta luego, pues si no me será dado regresar, si por lo menos espero que todos nos veremos en día no lejano allá, adonde nuestras fuerzas son necesarias, para la verdadera consumación de nuestra independencia.

Aprovecho esta oportunidad para ofrecer a Ud. mis simpatias y felicitaciones por su labor en beneficio de la H. Colonia.

SS. y Atta. SS.

Ma. del Refugio Ramírez

Le deseamos un feliz viaje.

"HUMO" PROGRESA

El Club Deportivo que

SANDRA VALDÉS, INDIANA HISTORICAL SOCIETY

Letter from María del Refugio Ramírez from Mexico to the Mexican colonia *in Indiana Harbor. The letter was published in the Latin American newspaper,* El Amigo del Hogar, *October 1928.*

Irene Osorio

Irene Osorio's family, the Figueroas, were the owners of the Figueroa Print Shop, which published newspapers for the Latino community in Indiana Harbor. Irene has worked in education and human resources. In this interview excerpt she discusses mutual aid during the Great Depression and how the community survived discrimination. She also explains the founding of the *Latin Times* newspaper in the 1950s.

Date of Interview: July 28, 2017 | Age at time of interview: 68 years | Interview transcript audited by Nancy M. Germano (2017–18)

Mutual Aid during the Great Depression

NML: I'm curious about the 1930s, during the repatriation, where people who are voluntarily or involuntarily sent back to Mexico. What did, you know, what did they say that the community was like at that time?

IO: *It was very—from what I understand—very supportive of each other, and it was—they wanted to help each other as much as they could. And so, again, they would rent or do the bartering, that sort of thing.*

One good thing that my mom said that I remember is that the train—that the coal train that takes the coal into Inland Steel on those tracks back there by Block and Pennsy—people used coal to warm their homes—and the people from town—the little harbor area—would go by the tracks to pick up the coal that was falling off the train.

But my mom says that it wasn't falling off—that the men were shoveling the coal off so that people could get some because it was just, you know, it was car after car—railcar, railcar—coal, coal—and it's just going to get burned up to make steel, and these people needed some warmth. Some—certainly it wasn't excessive where they would get in trouble, but it was enough that people could pick up and load buckets and take home and put in their little stoves. . . .

I can remember people saying that they were frightened a bit because with the repatriation, it was not always voluntary. Sometimes people were just kind of snatched and put on the trains, and they were gone. . . . So they were—there was a little bit of alarm, there was a sense of fear, and I think (pause) people tried to—as I said, you know, support each other, help out where they could, and money was getting tight. I think once—when the strike was over, I don't know—if it coincided with the end of, you know, with the Depression and that sort of thing,

but I know that it got to be more difficult for folks because then they started feeling the discrimination.

But once they were in the community and they liked it, that's where they wanted to stay, and so—they wanted their church, and they wanted their community center, so to speak—you know, someplace where they could congregate and be with each other and share their food and their traditions and that sort of thing."

Discrimination and Community

IO: *My mom had noticed some women walking with slips on and a sweater over their shoulders. And she was surprised that they were walking down the street like that, and so she went to them and said, "What," you know, "what are you doing? What are you wearing?"*

(Laughs) And they said, "Well, we just went to Miravich, and he sold us these dresses very inexpensive, and they're very pretty."

And they were, and they were lacy. And my mom said to them, "Those are not dresses. Those go under the dresses." And so she went to Miravich herself to tell him to stop selling that to the Mexican women like dresses. And, you know, she didn't speak English very well at that time, but it was—she was so angry.

NML: She wanted to get her point across.

IO: *Yeah, and I remember too, she told a story of a woman who was in the butcher shop—a Hispanic woman—Mexican woman—and she wanted tongue."*

NML: Oh *lengua*.

IO: *And she was trying to get that across to the butcher, and she was standing there, and the man was like, "What are you saying, what are you saying?"*

And the woman was going, you know, she put her thumbs up to her forehead and put her fingers out like making horns. And she's going, "Moo," and she's pointing to her tongue.

And so the man was, like, laughing at her. And saying, "What? What?" And also making her say it—Yeah, and do it again and again.

And so finally, my mom went up there and said to him, "Tongue! You no speak English? Tongue!" (Laughs)

But yeah, it made me feel sad to think that, you know, people would be like that cruel like that. But I guess that's the way life is—things haven't changed that much. . . . No, but it was such a small—there weren't that many butchers around there.

Opposite: The front page of this Latin Times *issue of May 4, 1963, features a political cartoon by Edward Medina.*

LATIN TIMES

THE MIDWESTS MOST POPULAR SPANISH ENGLISH NEWSPAPER

LA FORTALEZA
Nopalitos al Natural
V. F. GARZA & SONS

VOL. VII No. 19   5¢   May 4, 1963

10 Teacher Jobs Open in East Chicago

The East Chicago public schools will employ an estimated 475 teachers for the next school term. All except 10 of these positions were filled Monday night as teacher contracts were approved by the Board of Education.

All teachers currently employed were rehired, according to Supt. Dan Simon.

The new tenure teachers are Constance Bazil, Mrs. Willie Dowson, John Dobak, Mrs. Marjanna Erwin, Henry Gillis, Ann Harrell, Mrs. Hattie Leonard, Myrtle Lewis, Barba Lovin, Norman Marsh, Ellen Mellady, William Morris, James Mulcahey, Donald Palla, John J. Patrick, Estella Reed, Mrs. Gladys Russell, Alex Sarkisian, Margaret Smith, Marie Spanos, Mrs. Alma Taylor, Barbara Webb, Mrs. Maxine Winbush, Theresa Wojaszek and Lucille Zitko.

NEW ADDITIONS to the staff hired Monday are: Mrs. Barbara Donnelly of Cleveland, O., primary; Sandra Hunt of Munice primary; Mrs. Mildred Stephens of Mississippi, primary; Lawrence Wier of Hammond, mathematics; Adraine Sabik, also of Hammond, primary; Mrs. Sandra Gray of East Chicago, kindegarten-primary; Dan Orlich of East Chicago, health and physical education; Dianne Sarkotich, East Chicago, English, and Jean Springsteen, of East Chicago; language arts.

Editor's Note:

This employment of teachers is well and good for the city and our children in general, but notice the lack of Latin names in the group that was hired

This policy is the policy of a man who asks for the Latin vote, our only answer can be, VIVA NICOSIA!

Mr. George Lamb appears to be up to his ole tricks again.

A few years ago, he made the front pages of the newspapers just before election time. He charged that some property owners had hired some hoodlums that beat him up.

(Cont. pg. 2)

COMENTARIOS SOBRE POLITICA
por Victor Manuel Martinez

En estos días está por culminar la campaña política que ha mantenido en tensión a los candidatos y partidarios que esperan triunfar en las elecciones del día siete de mayo actual. Sería aventurado decir quienes serán los triunfadores, ya que parece ser que los ciudadanos al contrario de otras ocasiones, han estado tomando un vivo interés por hacer que gane el o los candidatos de su predilección. Sin embargo, el hecho de que un Alcalde se haya sostenido en el Poder por espacio de once años, como así lo ha hecho el señor Walter M. Jeorse, nos da la probabilidad de que en estas elecciones resulte derrotado por su oponente el DR. JOHN B. NICOSIA, quien en su programa de trabajo ha incluido medidas justas que se pondrán en práctica con el firme propósito de beneficiar al pueblo. Por otra parte el Dr. Nicosia se ha dirigido al sector hispanoamericano y le ha ofrecido que nombrará como JEFE DE UN DEPARTAMENTO MUNICIPAL, a un descendiente de hispanoamericanos. A más de esto ofrece llevar a efecto un plan de urbanización que a la vez que embellezca a nuestra ciudad, beneficie a las clases sociales, sobre todo a las desheredadas y en las cuales queda incluido el sector hispanoamericano que es uno de los que más se ha abusado y se sigue abusando en todos los medios comerci-

ales, financieros y oficiales. Las promesas de NICOSIA son alentadoras, y la sinceridad conque ha principiado su campaña, son señales de que cumplirá con su programa de trabajo. Ojalá así sea.

En relación con lo que Mr. Walter M. Jeorse, Alcalde de East Chicago, ha manifestado en su programa, nada en concreto se puede decir. La experiencia que nos ha dado su actuación como Alcalde y político, nos ha hecho ver en él al hombre voluble, al político de dos caras, al individuo para quien los principios morales e ideales humanitarios no han contado, ni cuentan ni contarán. La propaganda que en favor de Mr. Jeorse hacen sus partidarios es falaz, carece de toda sinceridad, y es por tanto mezquina y vil; convenenciera y odiosa. Para demostrar lo anterior bastenos ver y estudiar la condición, posición e intereses que han ido creando en el Gobierno Municipal, los que hablan en favor del Alcalde Jeorse. Estos mismos son los que han cooperado para que el sector hispanoamericano siga siendo víctima de atropellos y discriminaciones. Si a esto llaman JUSTICIA SOCIAL los partidarios de Jeorse, pobre de nuestro pueblo.

A los hispanoamericanos en tiempos de elecciones como en tiempos de guerra se les dice que deben pensar y actuar como americanos, y no como un grupo minoritario, esto lo aceptan los prejuiciosos en estas ocasiones; pero en realidad ¿quienes son los que hacen las divisiones? Acaso no son los que creen en la discriminación racial? ¿No son estos los primeros que arrojan a los barrios insalubres, áreas donde se

(Cont. pg. 8)

Probably the "butcher block" (laughs)—the guy down on Main Street (laughs)."

NML: So, what else—what other stories do you remember? I think—I don't know if I read in one of the articles you gave me or—talking about—oh, how they created their own movie house.

IO: *Yeah, they finally were able to get a theater—La Cuauhtémoc which was for Mexicans only, and they had Mexican programs. They had people like Cantinflas—films by Cantinflas and Jorge Negrete would be on stage—on the film singing.[57] And people loved the fact that they were able to, you know, enjoy that and hear it in Spanish, but they were not allowed to go to the Indiana or to the Garden.[58]*

Latin Times *and Latinos in Politics*

NML: When did the *Latin Times* start?

IO: *I would think it was like 1962 or so. I remember Kennedy–Nixon time period, and they would have articles in that paper about them.[59] So, I think was in that time period. And Nicosia was mayor in East Chicago and then Pastrick, so in that—oh, and there was another—Jeorse.[60] Oh, yeah, there were some political stuff going on that didn't make the printing shop or the newspaper very popular with Jeorse. . . . Actually, just that they were using the Hispanic community, and—"*

NML: Oh, felt that they were being exploited? . . . For the vote? So it wasn't, I guess, a genuine politician.

IO: *Yes, a genuine appreciation for the community—no! It was one just to use for the vote, and then you're done—and promises made and not kept and things of that nature—and the newspaper would call them out on different things. And they were not too popular with Jeorse or with Nicosia. Nicosia, a little better, and then Pastrick, I think, because he was in there so long, they started out hopeful, and then it was just deteriorating because it became very obvious that he was going to be the mayor for like fifty-five years—no twenty years (laughs).*

NML: Yeah, it was going to be the political machine that he was (laughs). So, who started—who started the *Latin Times*?

IO: *My brothers. . . . It was Frank and Gus and George and Willie—my brother, Louie, later, and Louie was the one that kept it running towards the end. But the others kind of peeled off to support their families because they all had six kids except Louie. Louie just—it was he and his wife, so it was easier for him to live off whatever was coming in from the printing shop than to have all of them trying to take money from that and support themselves. . . . No, there were—oh it was definitely a community thing. I think almost everybody in Indiana Harbor had their name in the paper for something or other. And it had a little gossip column. So, "Hello, my name is Tillie," and for the very longest time, it was a big question in the Harbor. "Who is Tillie?" Because Tillie—*

NML: Oh, so Tillie was a pen name. . . . So, who was Tillie?

IO: *It was my brother George (laughs). And people would say, "Oh, I'm Tillie."*
And my brother would say, "Really, well what do you—?" And so he would just listen.
Then it—and for—it was a well-kept secret for—because the things that he had heard, you know, if people knew he was there, they probably wouldn't talk the same way and so that's, kind of, how the gossip stuff came about. . . . Oh, like how so-and-so graduated from high school; my daughter's getting married—"

NML: So, nothing malicious—just more like word on the street—

IO: *Oh, no, no, no. Just, yeah, this is what's happening. . . . And then the way it would end in—when you finally see those newspapers, you'll see it—and at the end, it would say, "Well," you know, "here's wishing everybody luck and so do I. And my name is Tillie." So that's, kind of, how it closed out. There was another column in there "Nickie's Quickies." And that one seemed to be a little more spicy because—I'm not certain where Nickie was hanging out, maybe more the bars (laughs)—but that one—and then a gentleman by the name of Victor Manuel Martínez would—he would write political columns. . . .[61]*
He did some really strong political articles, and I think those were the ones that really got to Pastrick and the other political officials.

NML: So, kind of like, "Listen up and answer" those, I guess, those "concerns"?

IO: *And he—he was well-educated, so his English, you know, he knew what he was saying, and he wrote it very well, and they couldn't deny what he was saying. They would always. . . . That's right. They would threaten—oh, this, that, and the other, you* *know—libel—but there was nothing they—it was the truth. This was there. They were careful about that.*

NML: So, I know like, in the sixties there was a local—like, we think is the first Latino-elected Latino official, Jesse Gómez. . . .[62] And so, do you think the *Latin Times* helped in his campaigning, you know, getting the word out?

IO: *Well, I know they printed things for him (laughs).*

NML: Oh, in terms of, like, signs?

IO: *Right, right. I imagine that they did because, again, it was an effort to help Hispanics get ahead in the community. But yeah, he couldn't have gotten ahead without the help of all the Hispanics in East Chicago.*

And I think people were proud of him—genuinely proud of the fact that he got into the political arena like that. And hopefully, you know, was able to do things for the community. And, you know, he was a very nice man—very well respected.

And I think his son—one of his sons and a, maybe, nephew are—his son, Jesse Junior, I think was involved in politics—whether he's in it now or not I don't know, but another—the nephew Gómez—I forget his name—I think he just recently retired, and he stayed in it more.

NML: Who else worked at the paper?

IO: *It was family—all family, except for the folks that I mentioned there. And we had a cartoonist. Now everybody did these things for free. So our cartoonist, Eddie Medina, he added a real nice punch to those political articles.[63] And he could make (laughs) fun of a lot of people—the mayor or whoever, you know, like they're catering for. I remember one cartoon, you know, catering for the Hispanic vote, and there's the mayor—because he was a very good cartoonist, and Eddie could actually make you see the mayor's face on this cartoon because the resemblance was there, wearing a Mexican sombrero, like, you know, "Here I am," with the maracas and all in that one.[64] Indeed, that was not—you know, it was, he was Mexican for a day, and that was it.*

And so, people contributed their talents, and I think—I believe they felt pretty good about being part of that, and it was nice. It was—the paper was—had critics and had people that liked it, but I think what made it, probably, stay around longer was the fact that it was really community information. Again, as I said, you know, people getting married and weddings and dances and things like that.

NML: Yeah, because the community was fairly large. I guess, larger than—in that time, than in the 1920s. So, when it was *El Amigo*—and so, it's probably, kind of, a way to, kind of, keep the community still together to, kind of, re-create that closeness—relationship—well, I guess, with the second generation for the first generation.

IO: *Um-hm. El Amigo was giving a lot of information about what happened in Mexico, what was happening after the revolution and the people had left, and it gave information about what was happening in this country as well, and in the community, you know—let's organize or, you know, collect money for a church, let's do this for so-and-so, and let's—so they had a broad picture, and then, of course, focused on what was going on in the community.*

The Latin Times was not broad in that sense. I think the only time they got more national was for the Kennedy–Nixon election. Otherwise, it was just local, and there was plenty of stuff going on in politics in East Chicago, and then, of course, the community itself—the people.

NML: Do you feel that—so, it's kind of during the era of civil rights. Do you feel like that's why the *Latin Times* came around because people were starting to have more of a voice or wanted to be more vocal?

IO: *It could be an awareness, you know, of what could we do, and I think the fact that we had the printing shop and had the equipment for a newspaper made it a lot easier, and people would joke around, "Hey, we should start a paper. We should do this. We should do that."*

And so, they finally got to doing it, and I guess they had things to write about, but I can't say that—

NML: That was the sole reason.

IO: *Right.*

NML: It was just, kind of, in the spirit of the time and then Kennedy—the Kennedy and Nixon, you know, election was pretty contested, to say the least, but maybe that was kind of like their call to action that, kind of, you know mobilized the community once again.

IO: *I would—and I think that's a good phrase—um-hm—to let people know they had power if they stuck together, and that they could make some changes.*

Carmen Velásquez as Told by Her Children

Carmen Velásquez was born in Parsons, Kansas, to Mexican immigrant parents, and grew up in Chicago, Illinois. As a child, she contracted polio and spent most of her childhood in hospitals and convalescent homes until the age of fourteen. Observing the nuns and social workers at the facilities planted the seed for her future advocacy work. She met her husband Albert in Chicago, married him in the 1940s, and moved with his family to Fairmount, Indiana.

Tending to a growing family in the 1960s, Carmen began independently working with the migrant farmworkers of Grant County and their families. She attracted the local support of the Catholic church and became instrumental with a farmworker advocacy organization called AMOS (Associated Migrant Opportunity Services). In 1985 Carmen passed away at the age of sixty-four. Interview excerpts are of her children giving a posthumous interview on her behalf. Those present were Celestina "Tina" Masterson, Mary Margaret Velásquez de Bertram, Richard "Bob" Bertram, Charles Velásquez, Cathy Mitchell, and grandson, Zach Adamson.

Date of interview: June 25, 2017 | Age at time of interview: Carmen would have been 96 years old. | Interview transcript audited by Nancy M. Germano (2017–18)

VELÁSQUEZ FAMILY, INDIANA HISTORICAL SOCIETY

Carmen Velásquez at a migrant center, 1962

Recalling Mother's Early Community Work

CM: *She would just pack us up in the car, and we would go to migrant camps. And she would see what—she would talk to the people, see what they needed; and she would make—somehow, she would bring whatever they needed. If they had like three or four families living in a little one-room hut or something, she would bring clothes, she would, you know, talk to people—try to, you know. And we would go with her, and she was—she would just do this on her own, and this is—*

MMVB: *And then she was able to work with her Third Order of Saint Francis group, who would support her in this work. And they would go out to migrant camps, too. And by then, she had a small community of people—and this is a group of about ten people from the church who would be willing to take this on as a project, so to help her. . . .[65]*

But she just saw that these were people that needed help. And she could speak Spanish, so she was able to do things that most of our Anglo community could not do. . . .

Yeah, there just weren't families here, but she was able. And so, the Third Order of Saint Francis side of the Catholic Church—Saint Paul's Catholic Church—was able to lend support, and they could—people would be willing to go.[66] And they'd drive in. Sometimes we would, like, pray the Rosary with them at night, do little things like that, but it grew and grew to the point where they could put a notice in the bulletin to drop off clothes on her porch. Her porch became the first, like, Saint Vincent de Paul that—we didn't have one in town.[67] We just didn't have one. . . . Yes, and so what we do have is now called Saint Martín de Porres in town, and she started it—on her porch. . . . But, it started on her porch and especially for the migrants—for the migrant workers. And she elicited, of course, more support from the church, and even if our parish priest couldn't do a lot, there came a time. . . .

The Start of AMOS in Grant County

MMVB: *Oh, retired in South Bend. He [Name Unknown], before he became a priest, was a lawyer. But he, as a seminarian, he came and gave a summer working with Mom and the migrants, and he and she got together—I can still see them in the living room writing out the articles of incorporation for what became known—and they even thought of the name—A-M-O-S—Associated Migrant Opportunity Services, because Amos was a prophet in the Old Testament who had to do with agriculture. . . . And they incorporated this and got federal funds for it—later, and AMOS set up offices in many cities throughout the state of Indiana. And today there's still, I think, a perpetual honorary award given to somebody who does a lot for migrants in the state of Indiana in my mom's name—the Carmen Velásquez Memorial Award. . . .[68] And when it was granted way back in the eighties—she died in '85, and it was after she died—it was the first time they ever did an award for a woman or a Hispanic—in honor of a woman or a Hispanic in the state of Indiana. It was Governor Orr, I think—Orr, yeah.[69]*

Farmworker Living Conditions

MMVB: *They lived there, and after Mass, people—it was just down the street from the church—they would—people would come there and have—just like we did today, a little food, a little cake, or something. And they'd have all the little children running around, and they'd sit there talking. And if it was somebody's birthday, they'd celebrate it, or whatever. And they started talking about—they're so worried, their families coming back up from Texas and their—they actually lived in the barns where the animals were. And they just moved the animals out and put the people in. And they never—year after year—they weren't supposed to do it; and they just did it every year because they wouldn't come check it till the people were gone. And, they'd say, "Oh, don't do that."*

NML: I've heard about people living in chicken coops.

MMVB: *Chicken coops—everything. And so, the people were just voicing their concern. And out of that sitting and talking—"What can we do? There's nothing we can do," they said.*

Benny [Benito] López said, "Oh, yes, there is something we can do!" (Laughs) "Let's go tell the governor that this is going to happen, and we don't want it to happen."

And it was Holy Week. It was—you know, there's two weeks of Holy Week—it was the first week of Holy Week.[70]

Protesting at the State House

MMVB: *So, we had gone to say, "You need to get migrants on your migrant subcommittee."[71] And we did a sit down, and we weren't going to leave, but we told the press we'd be there. So, that was on the PM news—the six o'clock news or whatever that night, and—*

RB: *The next morning the FBI was—*

MMVB: *The FBI was there. They said, "We told you to tell us if you're going to do something, you know (laughs). So, they were keeping an eye. And it turns out Mother's office at AMOS—one day Benny came in, and he (gestures) shushed his mouth. And he went to the telephone and he unwound things, and there was a bug in the phone. And he wanted people to know that they were being bugged and being listened—not, you know—it's in the office. So, anything you say in the office or on the phone would have been there, so it wasn't just made up. These things were happening.*

Sister Mary Soledad, Carmen Velásquez's sister, reading to several migrant children on a farm in Marion, Indiana, 1971

Figueroa for councilman poster, ca. 1959. Frank J. Figueroa ran for various offices in East Chicago from 1955 through 1975.

Chapter 3

Gaining Visibility and Power, 1970–1989

From 1970 through the end of the 1980s the Latino community expanded and also developed in new and important ways—geographically, politically, and socially. With new job opportunities, activism, and institutions, the growing community became more visible and powerful than ever before.

The Latino population in Indiana continued to grow in these years, not by leaps, but steadily. Consistent growth through the 1970s led to a population of 87,047 by the end of the decade. By 1990 the population had reached almost 100,000 residents. Latinos in Indiana at this time came primarily from Mexico, Cuba, and Puerto Rico. These national origins changed very little over the period, although the Cuban population declined slightly, likely because those who had been resettled by the federal government flocked to places like Miami with substantial Cuban communities. Although much of the Latino community remained concentrated, with almost half the state's Latino population located in Lake County, there was growth in new areas of the state, such as Indianapolis and in farming communities such as Grant County and others.[1]

As the twentieth century progressed, many of the state's Latinos found opportunity in increasingly diverse types of jobs. They could be found in law enforcement, higher education, politics, and other kinds of work. For example, Robert Salinas became the first Latino police officer in Kokomo, Indiana, in 1981.

ROSEMARIE I. GÓMEZ, INDIANA HISTORICAL SOCIETY

Mexican Independence Day parade in East Chicago, Indiana, 1981

"Christians by the grace of God; gentlemen thanks to our Spanish descent; noble lords from our Indian ancestry we are, then, the Mexicans."

"Cristianos por la gracia de Dios; caballeros gracias a nuestra descendencia española; nobles por nuestro linaje indio somos, pues, los Mexicanos."

"MIDWEST'S MOST POPULAR LATIN WEEKLY OF GENERAL COMMENTARY"

LATIN TIMES

VOL. XVI No. 19   FIVE CENTS   May 11, 1973

ALLEGATIONS, ACCUSATIONS NOTWITHSTANDING—

BALANOFF STILL LEADs

Local 1010 needs more stronger responsive leadership in order to assure that the steelworker gets what he has coming to him and what is rightfully his.

Of those who have announced their candidacy for president, the strongest, most able leader is Jim Balanoff of the powerfull Rank & File Caucus. Jim has shown that he will tackle problems and present his programs even on the international level. He has made the Board of the Inland Steel Co. face problems that they would like to handle better in close meetings or behind the Inland Steel Plant gates.

Weak, ineffective leadership robs the working man of proper incentive rates, fringe benefits and of other things that mean more money in the pocketbook. This has the effect of leaving the steelworker far short of what is rightfully his - In a sense of being robbed.

The weak, ineffective leadership robs the working man who in turn is robbed of independence and initiative who in turn is robbed by others higher up on the economic scale and so on.

Balanoff could bring back initiative and independence to the steelworker.

Hello! my name is Tillie

Are we going to let them knock us down again??? We have been battered, slammed, and knocked down over and over again. The one thing in our favor is that we always get up before the count of ten. We need support, we need people who are concerned enough to go to the **Council Meeting-Monday-May 14 at 7:30 p.m.** and show that they are uniting and not dividing the Latins. If you care, be there!! Let's show them that everytime they knock us down, we'll get up again and again.

---SPANK HANK---

Hank "the Baby" Lopez is trying to make a big jump from putting his mark on checks to a decision making position. I'm afraid it takes more than knowing how to mark your X on a check to handle your job. No sweat Hank, the "76" is still working good. I'm told you open your union rule book as often as your Bible. I believe you have an awful lot of reading to catch up on.

---O---

Tommorrow and tomorrow and tomorrow! Creeps in its petty pace...! Joe went down to see good buddy Klagger to lease a white on white on white Monte Carlo he was promised to be driving the car in 24 hours. Joe, waited and waited and waited...

At the end of the 8 weeks he figured the 24 hours were up. To make sure he shook his time-piece and his Mickey Mouse said, "Yea", you're right." Joe finally got tired and left the waiting room and went someplace else and bought a white on white on white Mustang Convertable. That's what I like, quick decisions.

---SPANK HANK---

Vince Kirrin is selling everything to the city of East Chicago but the LATIN TIMES. That makes for quite a bundle, Mr. Kirrin. Would you drink to that?

---O---

Hermelinda Gomez, 20, graduated from St. Joseph's College. She is studying to be a lawyer. Her father, Antinio is very proud of her and with good reasons, too.

Right on -- Hermelinda.

---O---

Mr. and Mrs. Ernesto Gonzalez and Mr. and Mrs. Cristobal Rodriguez wish to announce the marriage of their children Maria to Juan Daniel.

The marriage will take place on Saturday, May 26, at Holy Angels Cathedral at 2:00 p.m

---SPANK HANK---

(Cont'd pg)

If one were to look at it from the standpoint of the steelworkers its only a local union election. This June every local in the Steelworkers union will hold election of officers, so again what makes this particular local election so different from the others that will take place this June?

Probably the one big difference is the size; Local 1010 represents the largest local in the USWA it represents some 17,000 members. So when the international officers speak for its union members it would also like to speak for the largest local in the USWA. But, from the looks of past issues the membership of the local does not go along with its international officers. This local as so many others didn't even go along with

its district director. So the international would like to see officers who if they don't endorse international policies at least won't speak out publicly against them. Hence, the big push!

Local 1010 is one of the few unions that has 5 elected full time officers, because of its size and because it has the dues dollar to support it, it also has a lot of patronage. Some individuals involved in union affairs sometimes draw more from the union treasury than they do from the Inland Steel Co. that really employs them.

Some people if they "cooperate" receive "fringe" benefits from the international, from the industry and in all kinds of devious ways. Of course to receive these benefits they must be in a position "to speak" for the steelworkers. Some

"All that serves labor serves the Nation. All that harms labor is treason to America. No line can be drawn between these two. If any man tells you he loves America yet hates labor, he is a liar. If any man tells you he trusts America yet fears labor, he is a fool. There is no America without labor and to fleece the one, is to rob the other.

ABRAHAM LINCOLN

people have learned the knack after numerous terms in office and are really going great guns. I imagine if they would happen to lose the prestige of their powerful offices they would consequently lose their "fringe benefits."

This is why so many who aren't even steelworkers are so concerned about the outcome of the elections at 1010. All types of pressures are being applied,

some people can't take it they quit or drop out, others can take it and they try to fight back. Like someone said "it's all part of the game" only it's not a game.

True strength does not depend on the size of one's biceps. It is related to a sense of purpose, the ability to think and analyze, the proper respect for human response.

Cover of Latin Times *newspaper, Indiana Harbor, May 11, 1973*

Rising Latino Political Power and Activism

In the late 1950s the Figueroa Print Shop in East Chicago, which had published the state's first Spanish newspaper, *El Amigo del Hogar,* returned to its dual purpose as a local newsprint publisher. The sons of Francisco and Consuelo Figueroa launched the *Latin Times*, giving a voice to the Latino community in Indiana Harbor by commenting on local issues such as gentrification, labor unions, and politics. The *Latin Times* is credited with helping elect Jesse Gómez, one of the first Latino politicians in Indiana, to East Chicago's city council in 1963.

In Lake County by the 1970s the political power of the long-established Mexican and Puerto Rican communities was rising within local labor unions and individual Latinos were being elected to local government positions. Other members of the Latino community found new ways to increase Latino visibility and power in the state through community organizations, advocacy groups, and new Latino publications. Still, they were not exempt from negative and oftentimes racist attitudes.

In reaction to one reported racist comment, Latino students, along with a multi-ethnic coalition including white and Black students, staged a walkout at Washington High School in East Chicago. The walkout, which included nearly six hundred students, began on October 2, 1970. It is likely that the students were at least partially inspired by the largely Latino-led student walkouts in East Los Angeles, California, in 1968. The walkout in East Chicago was set off by rumors that, in the process of enrolling two Latino students, the assistant principal had stated that "Mexicans are lazy and ignorant." Whether this statement was made or not is a matter of dispute; the belief that it was stated nonetheless provoked a strong reaction that eventually involved local politicians and protests on the mayor's front lawn. Ultimately, the assistant principal was not fired, but the event propelled many individuals into activism and community engagement.[2]

Activism through Latino Social Service Organizations

Some Latinos who came to Indiana during this period had a greater degree of prominence in the general society than earlier immigrants, but they struggled with some of the same challenges of adjustment. Reacting to their lived experience as well as to national trends regarding immigrants, Latino activism began to develop in Indiana. Just as happened nationally, Hoosiers in this era formed organizations to advocate for and organize farmworkers, many of whom were Latino. In addition, political action regarding

Large Latin crowd bunches on steps, hears spokesman announce written agreement.

Students lounge outside, in hall after 3-hour sit-in.

Latins Return To Class

By CHARLES STERLING
Times Staff Writer

EAST CHICAGO — Latin students returned to classes today as Washington High School Vice Principal Mitchell Baran was removed pending an investigation of his alleged racial slur.

There were reports, meanwhile, that teachers would take action to protest Baran's temporary ouster and that Washington Principal William J. Giannopoulos' resignation over the incident was rejected by officials.

Students were instructed at a Youth Advisory Board meeting Tuesday night to return to school, ending a 3-day boycott.

Giannopoulos said Washington attendance was "normal" today with 139 students absent including 52 Latins. About 44 per cent of the ECW population are Latin-Americans.

Nearly 600 stayed away from classes Tuesday at Washington and other schools, took over the administration center and won a guarantee of Baran's tem-

Other Pictures, Page 1B

porary removal and a bipartisan investigation.

They claim Baran said Latin Americans are 'lazy and ignorant' in an exchange with two women trying to enroll an out-of-town student.

BARAN IS TO BEGIN "detached service" at the administration headquarters during the investigation.

YAB spokesman Antonio Davila read a written agreement Tuesday afternoon to a crowd of Latins bunched on the steps of the administration building at 201 E. Columbus Dr.

The pact ended a day-long siege in which students invaded the first-floor offices of Supt. Robert Krajewski and Asst. Supt. Robert Segovia in a wall-to-wall demonstration against Baran.

The agreement specifies:
1.—Baran's removal from WHS during the investigation which Latins will participate in through YAB representatives to be named as soon as possible.

Continued on Back Page This Section

Boycotting students demonstrated wall-to-wall.

Students were "at home" in the superintendent's office.

Front page article about walkout at Washington High School in East Chicago by Charles Sterling in the Times *newspaper, Munster, Indiana, October 7, 1970*

Carmen Velásquez, Benito López, and AMOS staff joined others to march from Marion, Indiana, to the governor's mansion in Indianapolis to call attention to migrant farmworkers' rights in 1971.

other national Latino issues, such as electoral inclusion and educational equity, grew in Indiana.

In the 1960s the National Farm Workers Association, led by César Chávez and Dolores Huerta, organized in the American West and Southwest. This organization led unionization efforts for migrant farmers in those regions, but also cast a brighter light on farmworker struggles nationally.

Around the same time in Indiana, Carmen Velásquez began to go to the farm fields of Grant County, Indiana, asking migrant farmworkers about their needs. Carmen sought out donations and services for these workers and their families. As the number of farmworkers and their families' needs grew, so did Carmen's resourcefulness. Gaining support from the local Catholic church, she helped establish a charity center.

Then, in 1965, with the founding and incorporation of the nonprofit organization Associated Migrant Opportunities Services (AMOS), federal funds were available to establish regional information centers with paid staff in Indiana. By the early 1970s Carmen recognized that the needs of advocacy were greater than the needs of charity, so she worked with a local seminarian to open an office for AMOS in Marion, Indiana. The staff of the sub-east AMOS office in Marion was active in highlighting the needs of north-central Indiana migrant farmworkers. Staff visited workers in agricultural fields and packing houses to keep them informed about available services and to coordinate direct services such as healthcare.

Evaluating the living conditions of employer-provided camps was of particular concern. This was no small feat. In 1974 there were forty-two migrant camps across Indiana. At the height of harvest season, an estimated 18,000 to 20,000 migrant farmworkers were working in the state.[3] Camps largely consisted of multigenerational families. A Howard County health department report recorded seven active agricultural camps, ninety-four families, and thirty-three single males.[4]

Another group that worked with migrant workers in Indiana was the Migrant Ministry, presently the National Farm Worker Ministry. National in scope, this organization had operated in fifteen states by 1939. Prior to the funding of AMOS, Migrant Ministry groups worked hand-in-hand with church groups and were largely volunteer-led. Later, Migrant Ministry groups continued to work in their local communities alongside AMOS. Like AMOS, they worked to address the needs of safety training, education, health services, legal aid, housing, and managing daycare centers. In Johnson County, a Migrant Ministry group was formed by local churches in 1969 to work with the county's one hundred annual migrant farmworkers.[5]

In the two decades from 1970 to 1989, other social organizations emerged around the state, offering comprehensive programs aimed at serving Latino individuals and families through social services, educational programs, political advocacy, and community events. Some of the earliest Latino organizations formed in Northwest Indiana during the 1920s to provide mutual aid for community members and new immigrants. By the mid-twentieth century, Indiana Harbor's cultural and mutual aid societies had merged into the *Unión Benéfica Mexicana*. This consolidated organization continued to provide aid and cultural enrichment to area Latinos in the latter part of the century. Additionally, with the growth and diversity of the Latino population, organizations such as the *Hijos de Boriquén* association formed to support the Puerto Rican community.

Some new organizations put cultural affiliation aside to holistically address community matters. One of these was the Concerned Latins Organization, established to tackle issues of Mexicans as well as Puerto Ricans and other Latinos in the region. These issues included bilingual programs, urban renewal, housing, and affirmative action since these groups had traditionally been discriminated against.[6]

In Indianapolis, Latino organizational roots go as far back as 1969–70 with the founding of the *El Centro* Hispano-American Multi-Service Center, located on the east side of downtown at 617 East North Street, just blocks away from one of Indianapolis's earliest *barrios*, centered at the intersection of Pine and Market Streets. As the population and needs of the Latino community grew, so did *El Centro*'s services.

Clockwise from top left: Fred García of the Hispano–American Center speaking at Fiesta Indianapolis, 1981; Unidentified Nun, with migrant children in Marion, Indiana, July 1971; Dancers at Fiesta Indianapolis celebration, ca. 1980s

Meanwhile, as the Latino community expanded, so did organizations that focused on culture, education, and business. Fiesta Indianapolis held its first festival on Monument Circle in 1980. In the following decade the Hispanic Education Center was opened at the Marian Center of Saint Mary Catholic Church. The Hispanic Business Chamber in Indianapolis followed suit a few years later.

While these new organizations were growing, the city acknowledged the need for a centralized location for services for its Latino population. This led to *El Centro* becoming an actual service establishment known as the Hispano–American Multi-Service Center. It provided community services, and it also served the Latino community's social and recreational needs, hosting dances, Mexican Independence Day festivities, and rite-of-passage celebrations. Later it would evolve into a human and social services organization, specifically covering the needs that were being underserved by other local organizations. Thus transformed, the Hispanic Center operated at its North Street location until the early 2000s. As the twenty-first century dawned, at the request of some funders the center would be consolidated and merged with other entities to form the umbrella organization known presently as *La Plaza*.

As the social services for Latinos were being consolidated and centralized, Indiana's capital city was host to Latinos from many different countries. In August 1987 the United States hosted the Tenth Pan American Games in Indianapolis. The games were multi-sport competitions among athletes from the countries of North, Central, and South America, along with the Caribbean. Locally, this raised the profile of the cultural and ethnic diversity of Indiana's Latino community. Many local Spanish-speaking Hoosiers and their community organizations, such as *Sociedad Amigos de Colombia*, volunteered at these games.[7]

From 1970 through 1989, just as in previous years, Latinos in Indiana grew in population. But this era stands out for the movement of Latino populations into the interior of the state, for the new opportunities that Latinos enjoyed professionally and socially, for Latinos' growing activism and entry into the political arena, and for the organizations formed by and for Latinos from different Spanish-speaking countries in many parts of the state. It was an era of greater visibility and power for Latinos that came on the eve of the community's most rapid and dramatic growth.

History in Their Own Words: Stories from Gaining Visibility and Power

Raúl and Rogelia Piñon

Raúl Piñon was from the Mexican state of Jalisco and part of the Bracero Program. He began to work in the United States during World War II. While in Texas he met Rogelia, who was also from Jalisco. The couple married, worked, and started a growing family while serving as migrant farmworkers, following agricultural seasons from Texas to Michigan. During the winter of 1962 they decided to "settle out" of the migratory stream and live permanently in Indiana. The family would initially settle in Pumpkintown and later in Mount Summit in Henry County. Theirs would be the first Latino family to settle in Mount Summit. Raúl and Rogelia were accompanied by their son, Horace Piñon, and daughter, Hope Logston, for this interview. While both Raúl and Rogelia spoke some English, they mostly answered in Spanish and their children assisted with English translation for the purposes of transcription. This was the first interview conducted for the Indiana Latino History Project. Excerpts of this inter-

Feliciano "Felix" Espinoza, former owner of El Nopal *Market in Indianapolis (left), with Tulio Guldner (back), and Mayor Richard Lugar at the Hispano–American Multiservice Center, ca. 1970s. Felix and Tulio founded the center in 1971.*

view depict the couple's experiences as farmworkers, with discrimination, and with Latinos of different ethnic origins helping them to settle in Indiana.

Date of Interview: August 19, 2016 | Ages at time of interview: Raúl, 97 years; Rogelia, 83 years

Starting Work in the United States

HP: *The first time he came across the border was to work at a factory and at that time he was making 40 cents an hour. . . . And that was during the war.*[8]

NML: The World War II?

Raúl: *Sí.*

HP: *Yes. . . . Then he went back to Mexico and came back later with a contract with the gentleman from the United States to work in the field. . . .*

NML: Okay. And Rogelia, did you come to the United States. . . . When did you come to the United States?

HL: *She came to the United States with a card like a tourist card to be able to buy things here and go back. And she came with a cousin and her uncle and then her cousin went back, and she stayed, and that's how she met my dad at the restaurant. She was working at the restaurant, also. . . .*

NML: Okay [Raúl] How did you get your contract? Did they come to Mexico?

HP: *When he came over, he met the gentleman that offered him a contract because he was looking for men to work on the field, and that's how he got the contract offered to him by this gentleman to work on the fields.*

NML: And where was this guy? Where were his fields?

HP: *In Mission, Texas, the [Rio Grande] valley. . . . He was there as a farmhand basically, and he would help with setting up the irrigation in the fields and cleaned the produce, the vegetables, and just a hired hand around the farm.*

RAÚL PIÑON FAMILY, INDIANA HISTORICAL SOCIETY

Raúl Piñon (on right) and two other men pause during cherry picking in Traverse City, Michigan, ca. 1954.

Top: Rogelia Piñon working in a Brooks Foods field near Mount Summit, Indiana, ca. 1969; Inset: Raúl and Rogelia Piñon in their home in Pumpkintown, Indiana, ca. 1960

Traveling the Migratory Stream

HP: *He didn't really work that much in Texas once they started traveling around to the different parts of the country. The only time he would work in Texas [was] when they went back there because a certain crop was in season. So that's how they would go back to Texas, because their life was to travel the country, following the produce. So different times of the year, certain areas of the country, is when the produce is coming in. So they would travel all over the country and then come back to Texas when Texas produce was in season. . . .*[9]

The first time they left Texas was to come to Indiana. . . . They came to a canning factory; that was Brooks Foods, which is in Mount Summit. . . .[10] *They came to work in the fields, harvesting tomatoes. . . . So they would plant them, they would clean them, hoe the fields, and then they would pick them.*

HL: *And in the meantime, after they would plant and hoe the tomatoes, before it was time to pick, and they would go to Traverse City in Michigan to pick cherries. . . . And after the cherry was picked, they would come back to Indiana to pick tomatoes. . . .*

Raúl: [In Spanish]: *Texas, then right here in Indiana. I pick the tomatoes right here in Indiana. And when . . . before coming to pick the tomatoes . . . I went, I went to Michigan—Traverse City—to pick cherries. When the tomatoes is ready for the pick, come back from Traverse City to Mount Summit and pick tomatoes.*

(Laughs) I came two to three times to Indiana before deciding to stay here. The last time when I came back to Texas and the West Texas—for picking—cómo se dice algodón? (How do you say cotton?)

HP: *They would pick the cotton in West Texas. . . . So, after the third time coming back to Indiana, they used to go to Texas and to pick cotton, and they just decided that they would come up here and settle here in Indiana. . . . They went back [to Indiana]; they knew some people at the canning factory, and the canning factory had housing, kind of a trailer park area that they would have the workers that would stay there, lived there during the season. Well, when they got here in January of '62 the factory did not want to open up the housing just for one family. So, they were kind of just stuck there; and the gentleman that was living above a grocery store in Mount Summit, by the name of José Morales, has seen there the family, parked basically on the side of the road and decided to come and talk to them and see if he could help them.*[11]

Migrant Worker Housing and Living Conditions

HL: *The canning factory, they had about over one hundred little . . . red little houses like a one-room house, and that's where they actually lived in. And everybody had to carry their own stoves and whatever they needed because there were . . . just a little empty one little bedroom house, and they [Brooks Foods] had over one hundred of them like that. . . .*

HP: *There was this peak season, there would be about four thousand people that would come and lived there [in camps]. . . .*

HL: *Not so much in Pumpkintown, but in other little camps. And in town they would actually have like, they would have, there were trucks, vending trucks or whatever they would call them, and they would sell food for the migrants there.*

First Home in Pumpkintown

HL: *It was a main building in the front, and years ago it was said that used to be a stagecoach stop, and it had like different rooms towards the back, and that's where, in big house is where they stayed for a while until he was able to fix the rooms in the back, and we lived in those rooms.*

Experiencing Discrimination in Indiana and Michigan

HP: *The first time that they experienced discrimination was the gentleman that they had like a driver or a person that would drive them to different areas. That took them up to Muncie to get out just to get out and look around and see what was around. And they stopped at a dealership and he [Raúl] was just looking at automobiles at that point. The owner or the person that worked at the dealership came out and just point blank told them, "We don't want to deal with Mexicans here. . . ."*

They used to be a truck that used to, again, carry people back and forth from their home or wherever they were staying at to the fields or where they were working at. And once, one of the trucks used to have to cross through Muncie; and he was stopped at one point and was told that they didn't want to see him driving through there.

I guess the most, I would say most blatant discrimination that they themselves faced was up in Michigan when they were working up there on the cherries. And they went to a neighboring town and went to a restaurant to eat with the family and they noticed that nobody was attending to them. And finally, one of the waitresses came over and told them that they did not serve Mexicans in that restaurant. So, they got up and left.

Latinos Helping Latinos

HL: *There was a Cuban family that lived in Newcastle, and they were the ones that gave them the idea of getting their citizenship. . . .*

She was a lady that helped them when my mother was going to have her gallbladder appendix removed. They had no insurance and no money. This lady, her name it was María Oclander (points to photo).

Raúl: *This lady is from Argentina.*

HL: *And she helped them fill up papers so they could do surgery, emergency surgery on my mother and for the medical bills.*

Values and Work Ethic

HP: *That's one thing about dad, his work is always, work has [been] very important to him, as it has been probably to most Hispanic families. That's what he has instilled in all of us. I mean there wasn't an option of not working. It was always, you work, and you take care of your family and take care of your house. So that was always something that he instilled in all of us—that work is very important and hard work is very important. So that's one thing that he's always; that's why he retired at 88.*

Robert Salinas

Robert is a native of Corpus Christi, Texas. After visiting with his grandmother in Kokomo, Indiana, his parents decided to relocate to the Midwest in 1969. Robert would later work with his father at American Standard Pottery. He also worked for Chrysler Transmission Company for a while and was laid off during the economic recession in the early 1980s. After a chance meeting at a local gym, Robert was encouraged to apply for a position at the Howard County jail. Following this, he attended the police academy and was sworn in as a police officer in 1981. When he retired in 2016, he was the first and only Latino police officer in the City of Kokomo. In his interview Robert talks about his experiences moving from Corpus Christi to Kokomo, growing up in Kokomo as one of very few Latinos in the area, and his work as a police officer. *[Warning: This interview contains derogatory language.]*

Date of Interview: October 27, 2017 | Age at time of interview: 61 years | Interview transcript audited by Nancy M. Germano (2017–18)

Family in Corpus Christi, Texas

NML: So, what did they do? So, did your parents work while you were growing up, and what did your grandparents do as well?

RS: *Yeah. My grandpa—Johnny Salinas—he was involved in the produce business. So, he worked for Corpus Christi Produce Company, and he was, kind of—would go around different grocery stores or whatever, mom and pop stores, and get orders, and then the produce would be delivered.[12] And he got started in that business very—at a very young age. I know my dad and his brother Rudy—that was one of the things, you know—they really didn't get to do many school functions because Grandpa was always looking for them to get them in the old—I think it was a 1953 Chevy truck—to load them up so they could go and* collect cabbage crates, which were, kind of, made out of wood, and they would recycle them—and to be able to load them back up with different types of vegetables or fruits and deliver them to the stores. So, part of—my dad and his twin brother Rudy—was to help Grandpa, so you know, that was—and ultimately, my dad stayed in the produce business. He ended up getting a job as he got older at the Corpus Christi Produce Company, and then, he would make trips to Mexico to bring produce from Mexico to Corpus Christi. . . .

I know growing up some of my experiences was that I remember my grandpa used to take me—Johnny Salinas used to take me with him to go pick up orders in different parts of surrounding counties and cities within Corpus that we would travel. . . .

Yeah, absolutely. I mean, it was, you know, everybody knew everybody, and they knew if you wasn't from the neighborhood. You know, I remember that we lived in a neighborhood called La Cuarenta, which is the Fortieth. And then right at—Greenwood Street would separate the Fortieth Street to La Bolera—it was another neighborhood—it was called La Bolera. And my grandparents actually lived in a nicer part of Corpus—a little nicer part. So, in order for me to go visit my grandparents and ride my bike over there—I couldn't ride my bike through the neighborhood called La Bolera because of the gangs and fights. If they knew you were from the opposite neighborhood, like La Cuarenta where I was from or vice versa, they would try to harm you or fight with you or do, you know, for—so I would take my chances through Corpus Christi freeways trying to cross the bike—on my bicycle—to go see my grandparents. And through the grace of God (laughs), I was able to, you know, find my way through and cross and back and forth. I'd done that quite a few times. I spent a lot of time in the beach, you know, in the bay front there at Corpus—Padre Island, Oso Bay, Pelican Bay, Port Aransas, Aransas Pass. I rode my bike in a lot of those areas and done a lot of fishing. My dad would take me fishing, and we'd go out on a boat or—there by the bank and fish.

Moving to Indiana

RS: *But, yeah, as we moved to Corpus Christi, and we left the beautiful city, like—I mean, we moved to Kokomo, Indiana. We left the city, Corpus Christi, which is an ocean—you know, the gulf there—to—we have a creek running here. And I call it the "Sparkling City by the Creek: Kokomo, Indiana," you know what I mean (laughter)? . . .[13]*

Nineteen sixty-nine. It was in 1969 when my mom and dad—and the reason we moved up here was because my mom hadn't seen my grandma, Irene, because she had divorced my grandfather, which was Tony Amaro—my mom's biological dad.

Robert Salinas (front) with his grandparents, Beatrice and Johnny Salinas, in Corpus Christi, Texas, 1961

And my grandma married another man, and they had several children, but he was a migrant worker, so they were up in Indiana.[14] And my mom had not seen my grandma for several years, and she knew that they were out here, so they decided to take a vacation and come to Kokomo, Indiana, at a migrant camp to visit my grandmother. And Dad decided that he wanted to stay here to, kind of, move away from the neighborhood that we were at. So, you know, we ended up settling here—ended up going

back and getting all of our stuff and moving in a duplex apartment. And then, I just tried to get used to their schools and the way of doing things and, you know, I mean, I remember being called different names—you know, racial names. . . .

They were spread out. There was not a specific area where Latinos would, you know, want to move such, like, a neighborhood or, you know. They were spread out, and these families here had been—a lot of these families had been here for quite a *while. So, you know, I—the culture shock for me trying to go to school—twelve-year-old kid trying to go to the schools here—there was—it was a little rough and, you know—I mean, I was being called certain, like, racial names, you know, that I never heard growing up in the Mexican neighborhoods, you know? We didn't call ourselves spics or wetbacks or whatever, you know? I mean, I guess, you know, when they would say some of those names, I would kind of laugh and stuff because I really didn't know what they meant until, you know, after a while. It didn't take me too long where I realized that, you know, they were racial names and being derogatory towards my nationality. But anyway, you know, I went to school here. I ended up going to Kokomo High School—graduated from Kokomo High School.[15] During—at Kokomo High School, when I went—I was going to the high school here—there was some rioting. . . .*

Actually, I had heard a lot about Kokomo. You know, Kokomo apparently from little—some of the history—was one of the main areas where they would congregate, you know—at Elwood, Kokomo—and that kind of thing. And I had heard about the Klan.[16] I really didn't experience the Klan until I actually became a law enforcement officer—police officer. I was involved in, you know, Klan rallies and those kind of things as protection to make sure to keep the city safe or whatever.

Agricultural Work, Workers, and Families

RS: *Yeah. My dad had no ambitions of returning to the produce. Our involvement with produce and vegetables and stuff like that was going to Mexico and picking it up and delivering it from the warehouse in Corpus Christi, Texas. We were not actual migrant workers like my grandma was. So, I mean, we—as extra money—I did, you know, pick tomatoes. . . .*

Yes. Indiana is known for tomatoes, you know—growing tomatoes and cucumbers—pepinos, you know.[17] So that would draw a lot of the migrant workers here during that season to migrant camps, you know. And that's how a lot of them—I mean, that's how my grandma ended up, kind of, like, staying here. . . .

The living quarters to the migrant camps were to me—a best way that I can describe them—were like living in a shed, you know. It was, you know, some of the—obviously, a lot of them didn't have running water; there was just a certain stationary area where everybody would go and get their water. They were equipped, as far as the inside, with the mere essentials, like a stove to cook or whatever. And they were all together in one area. That way it would make the farmer come in and pick them all up in one area—drive in—so it was all in, like, a group and load everybody up that needed to go out to the fields. But there were a lot of them, and the living conditions were not the best. . . .

No, actually, I didn't see things like that, but they did have a school that was called Roosevelt School, I think it was.[18] Roosevelt School—where it was a certain time of the year where during, you know, school season was closed—the school was closed—it might have been during the summer—they would have—where they would take migrant kids—a lot of Hispanic kids—Latinos—there. . . .

And they would teach them, and they would talk about the things that were happening around the world, you know, like that Chávez trying to make things better, and they would give you a little bit about the Chicano Movement, you know, back then for migrant workers, you know, across the country. I would go, you know, just so that I could hang around other, you know, Latino kids and stuff but not because I needed to go, you know what I mean? . . . Yeah, I wanted to go, you know, and sit through it because some of them couldn't speak English very well or whatever. And I learned both languages growing up in Texas—in Corpus Christi, Texas—English and Spanish. So, you know, I mean—it was interesting.

Starting a Family

RS: *But I was ambitious. I mean, I didn't want to be, like—I was always—looked at myself as being somebody different. Even growing up in Texas with the gangs and everything that was going on, as somebody trying to—I don't want to be like this person, I don't want this kind of life, I want better or whatever for myself. And then, obviously, my daughter was born and I met my wife, and then I knew that I wanted things better. So, I never settled, you know. I left home when I was really young and lived with my wife. I wanted my own privacy. I wanted to be my own provider for my daughter or whatever. I didn't want to have to depend on my parents. . . .*

So, I was really young and, of course, didn't have much and worked at the pottery, and we lived off of that and—you know, very hardworking. I always wanted to get on, like, at Chrysler.[19] Chrysler was the place to work, because the benefits were better and the work wasn't quite as hard—not that I was scared of working, but—you know, working hard—but I was just—wanted to have a better job, you know. And I got on at Chrysler, but it was—back then, Chrysler and Delco here were the two main places that everybody wanted to get on because they were just good jobs to have.[20]

They had the steel mill that was (pauses)—you know, there was a lot of people that worked there. They had a huge turnover because it was very hard work or whatever. But anyway, I got on at Chrysler. And they would always hire people, and before you could get your ninety days, they would lay you off, and then call you back. So, it was a trickle way of being able to—working and not working or whatever. So (pauses), you know, I worked at Chrysler. I was laid off—still, you know. . . .

A group of migrant workers in a flatbed truck on the way to an agricultural job in Henry County, Indiana, ca. 1970

Career in Law Enforcement

(Meeting Bob Sargent, sherriff of Howard County)

RS: *So, I am like—yeah—so at that point, I mean, I am trying to think, "Well, what have I done or not done that I am supposed to do, whatever it is?" But he pretty much just started carrying a casual conversation with me, asking me where I worked, and I explained to him that I was laid off. . . . And he asked me if I was married, and I said yeah, and I had a daughter and things were kind of tough for me—whatever. So he asked me if I was interested in being a jailer at the Howard County jail.[21] And I had no clue what a jailer was, so he, kind of, explained to me that, you know, it was to take care of prisoners and attend to prisoners and their needs and that kind of thing. He gave me a rough description of what it was. So, I said, "Absolutely," you know, "I'll take, at this point, any job that I can, that I—" you know, I needed work.*

So he says, "Okay, well, come to the courthouse and come up to the"—I believe, might have been the—"second floor," he says, on such and such date, and, you know, "and then we'll talk some more. . . ."

Yes. No, there was no Latinos on the force at the time. I was the only Latino. It was just Black and white officers that were there, you know, in the interview board. So, there was a couple of times—it was kind of disappointing to me because I knew that there were—had some openings or whatever, you know—and I wasn't getting a call, you know. It discouraged me, and I now, I wanted it so bad—so bad, you know (sighs). So I was—one day, wife was gone, and I was at home, and I was pretty hungry, so I grabbed open the refrigerator (demonstrating) to make myself a ham sandwich, and I took a huge bite off that ham sandwich, you know—I mean, lucky I still have all my fingers. I remember that day because I was really hungry, and my phone rings—it was a wall phone—and the phone rings, so—

NML: Oh it's what you'd call a landline.[22]

RS: *Yeah, I pick it up—a landline these days—so I pick it up, and I got a mouth full of food, and I try to say "Hello," you know. And I hear this voice at the other end, kind of hard to hear, and I go, "Who is this?"*

And he finally tells me. He first says, "It's Peanut."

And I go, "Okay, well, uh, Peanut." Well, that was—back then, that was Rodger Fain—he was the chief of police for the City of Kokomo, and that's what they would call him—Peanut.[23]

So he says, "Is this Robert," you know, with this real low voice (demonstrates low voice), "Is this Robert Salinas?" you know.

And I go, "Yeah." I go, "This is Peanut—okay."

"Well, this is Peanut; this is Rodger Fain."

I still didn't know. At the time—even the interview—I had no clue who the chief was or anything. So, he says he's the chief of police, and so I didn't know whether to swallow or spit my sandwich out that I had in my mouth, you know—so I ended up doing a little of both, actually, so that I could clear my mouth to be able to talk to him.

And he said, "Well, I need you to meet with Captain Harrison because we need to—he needs to take you so you can do your physical."

And I knew that that was the last thing that you needed to—they would do before you would get hired—because I had to pay for the physical—to do—with all the other process that I had to go through. So, he says, "Yeah." He told me, he said, "We're thinking about hiring you. If you pass the physical, then we will, you know, go on and hire you."

So that was my start of my long law enforcement career.

NML: What year was that?

RS: That was in 1981.

Reflection on 2016 Retirement and Community Work

RS: *I was the first one in the city—or of the Kokomo Police Department—to be the first and still the last. I try to encourage people that hire them—to say, "You need to look around," I said, because I would be called in at the middle of the night when there were other Latinos that were in the area; they're passing through or visiting or whatever, that would commit crimes or [were] involved in something, you know. I ended up working a homicide case involving two brothers—one killed the other, you know—that didn't spoke very much English, so they called me in and then ended up investigating that. So, any time there's translation. . . .*

Greg Chávez

Gregorio "Greg" Chávez Jr. was born in November 1932 in Robstown, Texas. Greg's parents were migrant farmworkers who found and followed seasonal work. After service in the U.S. Air Force, Greg settled in South Bend, Indiana, working in business and education. In 1980 he began to work for the Bilingual Services Department of the

Robert Salinas (second row, center, with moustache) with fellow members of the Indiana Law Force Academy, 1981

Robert Salinas (in suit and beard) receiving Officer of the Year award, 2015

School Corporation of South Bend. After leaving the school corporation, Greg continued to work within the Latino youth population in South Bend and surrounding counties. In this interview excerpt, he discusses his work establishing bilingual programming at the South Bend schools.

Date of Interview: December 6, 2016 | Age at time of interview: 84 years | Interview transcript audited by Nancy M. Germano (2017–18)

Greg Chávez on Creating Bilingual Programming in South Bend Schools

GC: *Then I found a job with Bilingual here in town—Bilingual Department, School Corporation.*[24]

NML: So, was it the Saint Joseph County or the City of South Bend school?

GC: *South Bend (pauses). Myself and some other individuals, we went—in the late '70s—we went and talked to the superintendent, and we saw that the community—Hispanic community was growing, so we put in a request and talked to them—that we needed a bilingual department. And the superintendent saw, and he allocated five thousand dollars and got a consultant from Saint Louis, Missouri. And he came and evaluated the area and recommended that it would be good to have a bilingual.*

So, in '81—in '80, I believe, the school corporation trustees approved it, and in '81, they (pauses) went out and requested applications for a director for the Bilingual. Since '81 it's been in existence, and it's been a great, great help for the school corporation and the kids around here.

NML: So, what did you do in the Bilingual Department at the South Bend School Corporation?

GC: *I was the only male at that time, and I was working out of the main office. And whenever the director heard that she had a problem with the male students in any other schools in the school corporation, she would ask me to go and talk to the kids and their parents.*

NML: So, you were an asset (laughter) by being the only guy in the office.

GC: *(Light laughter) Yes.*

NML: So, is there any kind of moment in particular you remember about your career that sticks with you today?

GC: *Yes, in helping out the kids, you know. A lot of them were migrant kids, you know—they moved or come into the school. And that was my life, you know, when younger, when I was in Michigan. And I tried to help them, you know, talk to them, that school, it's nice to have. For example, myself, I would tell*

them—you know, at high school—and look what I did—nuclear weapons, electronics, which I never knew in high school or even in life. I didn't know what a plug, you know, on the wall—what kind of electricity it was and all of that. I learned that in the service, while I was cross-training—it's important. And then here in Indiana, they started—Governor Evan Bayh started the Twenty-First Century Scholar[s].[25]

I would make sure that, when they were eligible to apply for that, to make sure that they sign for it and explain to their parents because some of them didn't read or understand what it was. I would go home and explain to them—this is four years of free college money that you get, you know, for your son. So, they sign it, and I say, "He's got to make sure he stays in school, good grades, and no smoking, I guess, and no drugs, and all of that so—"

NML: Keep your nose clean.

GC: *Yes. So, I'm pretty sure I helped a lot of them, and while I was in Jackson Middle School, I was—then she put me down there.[26] I was to take care of the seventh and eighth graders—Hispanic students and anybody else that came in. They used to—a student bring some other kids, you know. And I used to—not all the time, but sometimes, I used to bring—buy some Taco Bell tacos, and we had lunch there in the classroom and go over some of the problems that they had, visit the classroom. The teachers would let me know—so and so, you know, is not speaking, not doing good work, and so I go and talk to them.*

Opposite: Greg and Rosa (Garza) Chávez on their wedding day, 1954

Poster for September 2011 Fiesta Indianapolis, held by *La Plaza* in Indianapolis

Chapter 4

A New Era of Growth, Diversity, and Advocacy, 1980–2020

Attendees at the Indianapolis celebration of Hispanic Heritage Month held by the Indiana Latino Institute in 2017 pour orange coloring into the central canal, temporarily changing the water's color in honor of the event.

NICOLE MARTINEZ–LEGRAND

1980s: Federal Immigration Reform

The rapid growth of the nation's Latino population in the 1980s brought immigration reform front and center. President Ronald Reagan's administration signed the Immigration Reform and Control Act in 1986.[1] While toughening laws around undocumented individuals and illegal immigration, this act notably reinforced border security and penalized employers for illegal hiring practices, affecting a wide spectrum of industries from agriculture to professional businesses. In contrast, the law legalized more than 2.5 million undocumented immigrants of all nationalities who were in the United States prior to January 1, 1982.[2] The Immigration Naturalization Service estimates that prior to this pathway to citizenship, there were roughly six million undocumented immigrants in the United States.[3] Also during Reagan's administration, Hispanic Heritage Week was extended to a month (September 15–October 15), and for the first time, a Hispanic, Lauro Cavazos, was appointed to the presidential cabinet as secretary of education.

1980–1999: Population Growth, Expanding Career Choices, and Public Health

The new millennium brought unprecedented growth in the Latino and Hispanic, or Spanish-speaking, populations throughout the state. In fact, more Latinos and Hispanics came to the state in the 1990s and early 2000s than in any period before. This growth included Latinos and Hispanics with a variety of backgrounds from across Latin America and Europe. While a large majority were still from Mexico, the number of nationalities represented was vast, including countries from South America, Central America, the Caribbean, and Spain.[4]

By 1990, Indiana had 98,788 Latinos identified in the census. This was about 1.8 percent of the total state population. Roughly two-thirds were Mexican; Puerto Ricans were the second largest group, representing 14.2 percent of the Latino population; and Cubans, who represented 1.9 percent of the Latino population, were the third largest group.[5]

In this era Latinos were working in a wide variety of professions, making strides in the areas of education, public health, and cultural awareness. Indiana Latino leaders were also advocating for their community in new and important ways, breaking boundaries and gaining notoriety outside of the state.

One prime example of a Hoosier Hispanic leader who made national waves is Gabriel "Gabe" Eloy Aguirre, owner and chief executive officer of Indianapolis-area-based SaniServ, an ice cream and frozen beverage machine manufacturer, whose machines could be found in fast food restaurants, hotels, and convenience stores.[6] Gabe was born in Ohio to Spanish immigrant parents and grew up in poverty. In 1955, after his military service and a short time working in Ohio, he moved to Brownsburg, Indiana, just west of Indianapolis, for a repairman job at SaniServ. From 1955 to 1977 he moved up the ranks from repairman to salesman, and eventually to owner and CEO of the company. In this position, Gabe was able to purchase SaniServ in 1977 from the General Foods company. He was ambitious in the 1980s, propelling SaniServe into European and Asian markets. Locally, he served as president of the newly formed Indianapolis Hispanic Chamber of Commerce. National recognition came to Gabe in 1988 when he was formally recognized by President Reagan as the National Minority Entrepreneur of the Year. From humble beginnings, he truly was a self-made man.

Recognizing education as the foundation for success, Gabe invested in the community by starting an education foundation in Brownsburg. He also supported local organizations such as the Hispano–American Multi-Service Center, also known as *El Centro* (the Hispanic Center). His local leadership of the Indianapolis Hispanic Chamber of Commerce would earn him additional national recognition with a presidential appointment as the chairman of the U.S. Hispanic Chamber of Commerce in 1991. By the mid-1990s Gabe had sold SaniServ and retired.

Along with such success stories, boundaries and cultural norms continued to be tested throughout the 1990s, especially with the HIV/AIDS epidemic. Latinos and Hispanics would be both widely affected and underserved. The immunodeficiency virus affected everyone regardless of age, ethnicity, or other demographic background. Indiana was already in the national spotlight due to Ryan White, a Hamilton County youth who contracted the virus through a medical blood transfusion. White served as a spokesman as his story challenged the public perception of who could be infected. Due to this national coverage, there was not a lack of information, but rather, a lack of outreach and education specifically geared toward the Latino community. By August 1992, there were 3,392 positive cases in Indiana, of which 8 percent were with people of Latino or Hispanic descent.[7] Addressing subjects such as sex and gender orientation was, and continue to be, considered controversial in Latino and Hispanic cultures. The addition of the topic of HIV/

Holy Cross College | Division III
Business and Communication

PRACTICAL LESSONS IN

SUCCESS

A MIGRANT'S JOURNEY TO LEADERSHIP
LIFE LESSONS: WORK, COMMUNITY AND SERVICE

Gregorio Chavez Jr.
Community Leader & Activist

Wednesday, September 27, 2017 ♦ *7:00 p.m.*
Driscoll Auditorium, Holy Cross College

A child of migrant farmworkers who settled in Grand Rapids, Michigan, in 1948, Greg Chávez served in the U.S. Air Force from 1952 until he retired in 1972. He and his wife and children then moved to South Bend, Indiana, where Greg first worked in business and then as an educator in the Bilingual Services Department for the South Bend School Corporation. In 2017 he gave a talk about his journey to leadership for Holy Cross College in Notre Dame, Indiana.

AIDS presented a new challenge. The Hispano–American Multi-Service Center immediately started to address this public health issue.

By 1990, as a result of *El Centro*'s work, its executive director, Mónica Medina, a third-generation Mexican American and Hoosier, would chair the Midwest Hispanic AIDS Coalition.[8] Before this epidemic, the multi-service center was mostly known for citizenship and English language classes, job assistance, and other direct social services for the Spanish-speaking community. *El Centro*'s approach to education about HIV/AIDS was holistic: focusing on destigmatizing the virus, addressing its systemic causes, as well as serving the immediate needs of the Latino and Hispanic communities. This approach was comprised of youth training, peer education, anonymous testing, and counseling.[9] One leader who was instrumental in this work was Chris Gonzalez, the center's education specialist. Chris was a local gay activist, who later left *El Centro* to start one of the nation's first youth LGBTQ organizations, the Indiana Youth Group. Mónica would leave and become a consultant and work on statewide issues related to public health.[10]

El Centro laid the groundwork in the 1990s on how to address a critical public health issue in the Latino community. Other organizations and public health educators would follow its lead. One Latina who continued this outreach and education was María Luisa Tishner, a native of Peru. She first worked for Wishard Hospital in Indianapolis as a bilingual HIV/AIDS public health educator, reporting to Aida McCammon, another Peru native.

In 2001 Aida and Mónica Medina would work together to start the Indiana Latino Institute (ILI), an organization

María and John Tishner (left) and Aida and Wally McCammon at Evan Bayh Fundraiser in 1990. María and Aida, both natives of Peru in South America, first worked together at Wishard Hospital in Indianapolis, where María was a bilingual public health educator.

focused on addressing through education the health disparities caused by alcohol and tobacco use. The founding of this organization was made possible through federal funding.

While many others were involved with the work of ILI, María would join the organization and prove herself instrumental because of her public health educator expertise. Utilizing both conventional and unconventional methods, she helped educate the Latino and Hispanic communities both in Indianapolis and in the wider central Indiana area. She extended her community leadership by contributing to a coalition of dedicated professionals focused on influencing public health laws. In the early 2000s this coalition was instrumental in the passing of legislation that banned smoking inside public places, including bars and restaurants. After this achievement, ILI's services grew and expanded to other forms of advocacy and educational empowerment of Latino youth. In 2020 María was appointed board president of the Indiana Latino Expo.

2000–2020: Growing Population, Opportunities, Activism, and Organizations

As of 2019 Indiana population estimates showed more than 489,000 Latinos living in the state, accounting for 7.3 percent of the total population. Latino populations in Northwest Indiana remained the most concentrated, but in sheer numbers there were more Latinos in Marion County, a shift that developed between 2000 and 2010.[11] In addition, certain counties, particularly Elkhart and Clinton, developed Latino populations well in excess of 10 percent of their overall numbers of residents. This was massive growth considering that Elkhart County had less than 3,000 Latino residents in 1990. In terms of national origin, estimates from 2014 show that Mexicans remained the dominant group in Indiana, with Puerto Ricans and Cubans also retaining significant populations, along with people from Central America, who represented 6.8 percent of Hoosier Latinos.[12]

In the northern part of the state in Saint Joseph County, Gregorio "Greg" Chávez Jr., a native Texan and Mexican American, would work as a community advocate in the Bilingual Services Department of the South Bend school corporation. Recalling the challenges of his school years as a child of migrant farmworkers, he diligently worked with the local Spanish-speaking children and their parents, connecting them to available programs and resources. In the 1990s, after the creation of a college bound program called Twenty-First Century Scholars, Greg continued his outreach, educating middle school children and their parents about the advantages of this program, which could help their children attend college with significant financial aid. After his retirement, he continued to educate area Latino youth about opportunities for learning and advancement, such as the Indiana Senate Page Program.

In the last quarter century, Latinos have continued entering new fields. Indiana has its share of homegrown talent, and it also attracts outside talent to a wide variety of fields, most notably aviation. Aviation has deep roots in Indiana with training programs at Purdue University and the aviation industry in Indianapolis. In 2014 Cuban American Mario Rodríguez, a seasoned aviation professional, became the first Latino executive director of the Indianapolis Airport Authority. Mario's leadership has garnered national recognition; he has been a presidential appointee to the United States Department of Transportation's Committee for Aviation Consumer Protection for two presidential administrations.[13]

Outside of aviation, 2014 surveys showed that nearly one-fifth of Hoosier Latinos were working in management, professional, or related occupations. Significant numbers were also found in sales and office occupations. However, the largest share of Latinos was working in the production and transportation industries as well as in the service sector. In addition, large numbers of Latinos continued to lack opportunities and a disproportionate number endured poverty.[14]

Added to the economic challenges of many Latinos, bigotry has remained a key struggle for the community during the twenty-first century. Hate crimes against Latinos increased 15 percent nationally in 2016, due to increased negativity about Latinos and portrayals of negative Latino stereotypes during the 2016 presidential election and afterward. Indiana was not immune to this. In March 2017 a group of Latino and Black school children from Indianapolis who comprised a winning robotics team in Plainfield, Indiana, were faced with a chant of "Go back to Mexico."[15]

Latinos have not simply endured this maltreatment. Just as in the past, they have mobilized and organized. In 2006 an estimated 15,000 people rallied in downtown Indianapolis demanding immigration reform, part of a national movement reacting to anti-immigration laws. Latinos played an outsized role in this movement. Similarly, in 2011, after Indiana passed an anti-illegal immigrant law (SB 590) that many believed would open avenues for discrimination against Latinos, the East Chicago-based organization *La Unión Benéfica Mexicana* joined a federal lawsuit to stop the law from going into effect.[16]

As the Latino population has grown and diversified ethnically and socio-economically, Latino organizations have responded by developing and expanding in new ways, including working statewide. ILI has continued to address issues important to the state's entire Latino population. Founded in 2001, it originally focused on health and education-related issues important for Latinos.[17] Each summer, ILI has also partnered with private, public, and non-profit organizations to offer undergraduate internships and fellowships in various fields of study. Students receive professional and leadership development training and participate in civic and community engagement opportunities during their participation in the program. ILI also has hosted the Latino Education Summit, an annual event that brings together 1,500 Latino high school students from across the state to inspire them that college is possible, to provide them with the tools and resources to navigate the college process, and to facilitate the exploration of colleges and universities through a college and opportunity fair.

ILI has not been alone in its work for Latinos. In 2015 ILI surveyed a list of more than one hundred organizations and individuals representing the myriad of ways in which Latinos were serving and being served statewide. The median age of these organizations was twenty-two years, showing that many new organizations were developing in the twenty-first century. Most were nonprofits, but significant numbers also included educational, faith-based, and governmental organizations. Among them were *Fuerza Latina* in Vanderburgh County, *La Casa* in Elkhart, and *La Plaza* in Indianapolis.[18]

La Plaza formed in the early 2000s from longstanding organizations such as Fiesta Indianapolis, the Hispanic Education Center, and the Hispano–American Multi-Service Center.

Supermercardo Mexico *in East Chicago, Indiana, 1999*

La Plaza continues to offer services that were offered by the Hispanic Education Center and *El Centro*, while Fiesta Indianapolis continues to serve as the city's premier annual Latino cultural event as well as a fundraiser for *La Plaza*.

Meanwhile in Evansville, a group called HOLA, or Hospitality and Outreach for Latin America, was also established in the early 2000s. This organization has worked on a variety of issues, organizing and empowering Latinos in the southern part of the state by starting an annual Latino festival. Some of its initial founders were longtime area residents from Venezuela such as Maura Robinson and Alfonso and Daniela Vidal.

Above: HOLA (Hospitality and Outreach for Latin America) Parade in Evansville, Indiana, 2005; Right: Immigration reform rally in Indianapolis, April 10, 2006

From 1990 to 2020, communities of Latinos existed or developed in all of Indiana's major cities and in a number of its small towns. They contributed expertise to the state's many high-tech industries and public health, worked as entrepreneurs creating jobs and economic growth, added culture through cuisine and the arts, and worked in the production and service sectors. As the twenty-first century continues, Latinos will help to define what it means to be a Hoosier—just as they have for generations.

History in Their Own Words: Stories from a New Era of Growth, Diversity, and Advocacy

María Luisa Tishner

María is a native of Peru; she lived and worked there for the early part of her adult life. A chance meeting at work with an engineer for Indianapolis, John Tishner, would change the course of her life. After a long-distance courtship and a relocation to New York to be close to her sister and learn English, María married John. Together they moved to the west side of Indianapolis and later to a neighboring town. John traveled internationally for work, leaving María to acclimate to a new country and environment on her own. She quickly found other Peruvians and Latino cultural groups in Indianapolis. After her daughter was nearly grown, María re-entered the workforce, serving as an HIV/AIDS educator for the Latino community at Wishard Hospital. Later she would continue her public health education career with the newly-formed Indiana Latino Institute (ILI) and work on a public education campaign about smoking cessation. Through this work, she and others have advocated for laws to outlaw smoking in restaurants and bars in Indiana. María continues her work with the Latino community through outreach with HealthNet. Her interview recalls her early experiences in Indiana and the growth of the Latino community.

Date of interview: November 4, 2016 | Age at time of interview: 60 years | Interview transcript audited by Nancy M. Germano (2017–18)

First Experiences in Indiana

MLT: *So, it was difficult for me to live in Indiana, because I have all my friends, my support. I, as a Latina, I like to be around people to talk to her [my?] friend[s]. So when I moved here, a month later—the move to Indianapolis—John went to Nigeria.*

María Luisa Cavassa Mesías standing in front of Honda del Peru where she worked in Peru, South America, ca. 1975

María Luisa Mesías and John Tishner in Peru before marrying in 1983 and moving to Indianapolis.

And I remember, he said, "Okay, here is the supermarket, here is the doctor in case you get sick, and here is your church." I went to Saint Christopher. . . .[19]

And because I didn't have any friends, I went to church on Sundays. And the masses at Saint Christopher started eight o'clock, nine, ten, eleven, twelve. So, if I went [at] eight o'clock, I stay there for all the masses. And I remember one time, the priest—some—Father Michael come and said, "I see you here. You can go. So, what are you doing? . . ."[20]

And I was so stressed out, and I start crying.

He say, "Come on, come into my office. What's going on?"

I said, "Well, I just moved from Peru. My husband is not here. And I don't have any friends."

And he said, "Well, there is a school on Washington Street. They teach you English, and then maybe you can have some friends." I can't remember the name.

Early Peruvian Community in Indianapolis and Peruvian Association of Central Indiana

MLT: *Right. The—that was keeping me connected to my friends and my roots and my food and my culture. So, we got together to celebrate the Peruvian independence, which is July twenty-eighth.[21] So, we called people, we find a place to get together, everybody make a dish. . . . And we come to celebrate. That is how each year we—and they also introduced me to*

Resident stresses Latino issues

By Tania E. Lopez
tania.e.lopez@indystar.com

Pike Township resident Maria Luisa Tishner remembers when she felt like an anomaly.

She moved to Indianapolis from Peru in South America in December 1983 after marrying her husband, John, a native Hoosier.

At the time, Indianapolis had few Latinos — only about 6,143, according to the 1980 U.S. census.

"I felt like one of the first ones," Tishner said, "and, little by little, I started to notice the growth."

Today, an estimated 65,000 Hispanics reside in Marion County.

As program director for the Indiana Latino Institute, Tishner, 54, helps coordinate programs on the dangers of smoking.

Having worked tirelessly along with a team of seven Latino Institute employees to help make Indianapolis smoke-free, Tishner is a member of the Coalition to Promote Smoke Free Pregnancies in Indiana and is involved in several other advisory panels in Marion and Hamilton counties.

Recently, the Latino Institute co-hosted a panel with the Latino Health Organization of leaders who work with the Latino community to discuss issues facing the community.

"We did other events but a panel discussion like that. It was the first time," Tishner said.

Panelists included Daniel Lopez of the Indiana Commission on Hispanic/Latino Affairs, who said communication among the Latino community and the organizations that serve them is not yet well established.

"We have to work together as a team," he told a crowd at the Marian Center location in Downtown Indianapolis.

Carlos May, the city's director of Latino affairs, echoed the sentiment.

"Sometimes the methods of disseminating information are not used properly. Each group is doing their thing, sometimes duplicating services," May said.

While panelists talked about what their groups are doing, the Latino Institute wanted to make sure they are on board with the institute's mission, Tishner said.

"We want to educate Latino leaders on the importance of Indianapolis being smoke-free," Tishner said. "In the Midwest, Illinois, Michigan, Ohio, Wisconsin and Minnesota are all smoke-free states. Why not Indianapolis? Why not Indiana?"

Tishner said the community has come a long way from when she arrived, and it's good to see that groups are coming together for a common cause. Still, in working with the Latino Institute, Tishner's mission is to continue to educate Latinos on the dangers of smoking.

★ Call Star reporter Tania E. Lopez at (317) 444-6044.

STEVE SANCHEZ / The Star

As program director for the Indiana Latino Institute, Maria Luisa Tishner, 54, helps coordinate programs on the dangers of smoking. She moved to Indianapolis from Peru in South America in 1983.

Article about María Luisa Tishner and her work at the Indiana Latino Institute in the Indy Star *from November 10, 2010*

Doctor José Tord. The doctor was the—he worked for—he was a doctor for immigration. So, every time that he received a Peruvian—so he send us the name, and said, "Oh, here, there is another Peruvian," so we can—so we called, and we keep the list growing and growing.

NML: So, how many—so, when you arrived here—so, what was it—1983 when you started connecting with the Peruvians?

MLT: *So, maybe in that room we were like seventy, eighty Peruvians. . . .*

Working with the Latino Community at Wishard Hospital

MLT: *It was a position from the Indiana State Department of Health that they gave it to Wishard, and Wishard contracted me.[22] So, I needed to educate twenty-five Latino youth—high school student[s]—about HIV/AIDS.[23] So it was that, and it was educating the community about HIV. So, I went to churches, I went to all of that. And I started working my first time in the United States.*

Early Start of the Indiana Latino Institute and Work on Smoking Cessation

MLT: *Yeah, I was working for that, and then Aida [McCammon] applied for a grant to do tobacco control for the Latino community in Indianapolis—in Indiana, so (pauses). She opened a—she got the money, and she found[ed] the Indiana Latino Institute, and then she come and approached me, and she said, "Are you ready to work full time?"[24] And by that time Marissa [María's daughter] was already in high school, driving, and all of that, so it wasn't a problem. And that's when I went and worked as a tobacco coordinator, something like that. And it was also to go and educate the Latino community about the tobacco and the second-hand smoke—the dangers of tobacco and second-hand smoke because, as you know, the Latinos, they drink and smoke, and they like to be with family—the kids, the grand—everybody in the same place smoking and drinking. . . . And in our countries, we didn't have the money from the Master Settlement Agreement to educate the Latinos, so the education start when they move here.[25] So—and to break the pattern— you know, the smoking was very strong—so it took us a lot of— many hours working and pass the ordinance.*

The ordinance in that time—when Aida—when we first got the money, we have ten Latino coalitions because we were with ten counties around the state. It was not only Marion County, it was Hamilton County, Tippecanoe County, Lake County, Porter County, Saint Joseph County, Marshall County (pauses),

Clinton County—I can't remember the other two. . . . So, we did the—some of the counties, I was also the person who was contact[ing] and see if they were doing their job (coughs) and also doing—here in Marion County, we help—we promote the ordinance. So, we work with kids in Hamilton County; we work with kids in Carmel, in Noblesville, in Westfield, Fishers. I have my group of kids that they went and talked to the city-county members. And also, we work with the city-county members here to pass the ordinance. We pass the ordinance. The first ordinance passed without the bars; and then we fought for the bars like four years ago, I think.[26] And we pass the bars.

NML: So, the ordinance was to stop smoking. So, we— wow!

MLT: *Um-hm, yeah. I was part of that movement. . . . The challenge was, for example, trying to convince—not convince, you know, to educate, you know. And just to go and to talk [to] them and to tell them how bad it is. We couldn't get through, so we needed visuals. So, I remember reading some of the educational material, and we went—we saw this lung—the pig lungs— and it was a healthy lung and a lung with cancer, and then it had been inflated. So, you have a pump, and you put one—the healthy one, and then you are trying to work on the sick one, and that was very impressive—very, very, very because it was visual. And then a lot of people, you know, "Oh, my God! . . ." Uh-huh. I got the lungs, and I went to churches, to schools, to churches, to schools, I mean, you name it—social groups—you go and you talk to them. . . .*

It was me, Aida, Marcela Flores, it was a lady from Mexico that—she did a wonderful job, too. She was very involved with the community; the people liked her. She is Mexican, and she worked for one of the radio stations. So, she was very, very good, and people loved her. And we did this, and then it was another—Amelia Muñoz, I think. She was the program director in that time. So, it was Aida, Amelia, me, Marcela, Óscar Morales, the manager. Morales used to be the—doing the cessation classes.

Greg Chávez

Gregorio "Greg" Chávez Jr. was born in 1932 in Texas to migrant farmworkers, served in the U.S. Air Force, and settled in South Bend, Indiana, where he worked in business and education. After working in the Bilingual Services Department for the School Corporation of South Bend, Greg continued to work with Latino youths in South Bend and the surrounding counties. In these interview excerpts, he discusses the Latino Students Page Program, receiving the Sagamore of the Wabash Award, and being a torch bearer for the Indiana State Bicentennial.

Date of interview: December 6, 2016 | Age at time of interview: 84 years | Interview transcript audited by Nancy M. Germano (2017–18)

Latino Students Page Program

GC: *Five years, and during that time I was working with some other teachers at the Bilingual. We found out about the Page Program, it was about ninety-two, I believe, when we started taking some seventh and eighth graders to the Page Program.*[27]

And after I quit, I still continued doing it—working out with the bilingual specialists in the high schools—I changed to the high school. So, we take anywhere from ninth to the twelfth— anywhere from five to ten kids from each of the high schools. I used to schedule four weekends or weeks with the Page Program and take each high school a different week with ten kids.

NML: Can you tell us more about the Page Program?

GC: *The Page Program is where they assist the state representative. Well before then, they have a history about the state capital, and they ask them how many state representatives there are, how many in senate, who's the governor or lieutenant governor and so forth—attorney general, all of those departments they visit while they were in the Page Program.*

NML: How long did you work with the Page Program?

GC: *I'm still working.*

GREGORIO CHÁVEZ, JR., INDIANA HISTORICAL SOCIETY

Greg Chávez riding in a Studebaker with the Indiana Bicentennial torch, representing Saint Joseph County in the state's Bicentennial Torch Relay in 2016

NML: So, you're still working with the Page Program, since 1992?

GC: *Yeah.*

NML: So, you take about ten kids every year?

GC: *Well more than that. Last year we took eighteen—three high schools. The year before we took about twenty-eight, I believe, or thirty-some kids. We go a day before and stay overnight. We take them to the mall—the Circle Mall.*[28]

NML: Oh, Circle Centre Mall. So where do you stay when you—?

GC: *In a hotel, motel, depending where I can find the best rates, and we spend the night—go on Sunday. And—now they change it to where they have the Page Program on a Monday. So, we go on a Sunday and turn them loose for two hours at the mall, and then we go to the hotel. Monday we come out and go to classes and return Monday.*

NML: Monday night.

GC: *Monday night.*

NML: So, they get kind of like training, and then they spend a whole day there.

GC: *Sometimes these kids—the parents don't have money to go on vacation. This is something like a vacation. Probably some of them haven't been to a hotel before, you know.*

NML: Is there any kind of memories about the Page Program, or kids who—?

GC: *Yes, I have met a lot of students, you know. They have gone through and then college also, and they come back, and they say, "Oh, hello, Mr. Chávez," and I don't remember them, but they remember and say, "Oh I was this," or "You're the one that took us to the Page Program," you know. And then we start talking, and sure enough, they have gone to college and—*

NML: Done great things.

GC: *Great things, yeah.*

NML: All thanks to your influence.

GC: *Yes.*

NML: So, you're still doing the Page Program?

GC: *Yes.*

NML: So, what time of year does that happen?

GC: *Right now they're getting started—it'll be sometime in February when we take them. There's a lot of paperwork and planning here and getting the names and submitted to the Page Program downstate and make arrangements—when we're going to be there, find out the dates, so we can make arrangements at the motel.*

NML: So, are they—so they're here for four weekends in a row?

GC: *They have it from January to the end of the legislative time—every week during that time—January, February, and sometimes when they go into March or April, I guess, sometimes—you can take kids. But you got to make appointments and select the day. Some—on regular times they only have a capacity of forty kids a day, but the Page Program now—they have a program for more than ten years that some Hispanic state representative started—Latino Students Page Program.*[29]

NML: Do you have just a Page Program for the Latino students?

GC: *Just Latinos. And last year, we only had fifteen high schools because of the snowstorm that happened. The year before they had thirty-one high schools—about 145 Hispanics from throughout the state.*

NML: So, you do the Page Program for the entire state of Indiana?

GC: *No.*

NML: Oh, you just do it for Saint Joe—Saint Joe, South Bend?

GC: *For Saint Joseph—South Bend only.*

NML: Okay.

GC: *But I go around—when I get the information, I go down to Goshen and Bremen and Plymouth and let them know, you know—because sometimes they—the people that took over the Page Program recently are sending just a note to the superintendent, and the superintendent sometimes doesn't send it down to the high school.*[30] *So, I find out the dates for sure because I've been doing work with them, and I call the Page office, and they let me know what date it is. So, I go then with that and give them the information for them to call the Page office or whoever is running the program—the Latino Students Page Program.*

Personal and Community Honors

GC: *I was selected to carry the torch for the Bicentennial for Indiana and also the—what do they call?*[31] *Council of the Sagamore—*

NML: Sagamore of the Wabash?[32]

GC: *Wabash.*

NML: So, when did you receive the Sagamore of the Wabash?

GC: *This year, on October twenty-eighth [2016], I believe—no, September twenty-eighth, because I got it before, and then on October seventh is when the torch went through South Bend, Saint Joseph County.*

NML: Do you remember what your route was from—what was—where did you pick up the torch, and where did you hand off the torch?

GC: *I picked it up here in South Bend, at Lafayette and Western, and the history museum, Studebaker Museum, donated a convertible, a Studebaker convertible.*[33] *And my destination was Bendix Woods Park, which is about eleven, thirteen miles from here. . . .*[34] *Yes. Bendix Woods Park. I traded with another person so that I would go through the Hispanic—Western, you know, business.*

NML: Yeah, the Western Street—when I pulled into town, I saw a lot of *taquerías* and—

GC: *And also in 1994, with the community help, I got a street named César E. Chávez.*[35] *It's the entrance to the Potawatomi Park here in town.*[36] *And then sixteen years later, we did another petition and asked the city to honor César Chávez on Western Avenue from Walnut to Falcon Street. I have about eight signs in between those streets—it's about half a mile, maybe three-quarters of a mile—placed on lamp posts.*

Miriam Acevedo–Davis

Miriam Acevedo–Davis was born in Moca, Puerto Rico. The year after her birth, her father would seek work in the tomato fields of New Jersey. Later he would bring Miriam and the rest of her family to settle in Brooklyn, New York. Growing up in Brooklyn, Miriam took advantage of an enrichment program called Upward Bound, shaping her pre-college and college experiences. After working, later marrying, and building a life on the East Coast, she relocated to Columbus, Indiana, with her husband in 1985.

Miriam worked in Columbus, and later Indianapolis, in organizations that provided services to the Latino community. In the early twenty-first century, she has been serving as president and CEO of *La Plaza*. In the following excerpts Miriam recalls her early experiences of Indianapolis and its Latino community.

Date of interview: December 14, 2016 | Age at time of interview: 64 years | Interview transcript audited by Nancy M. Germano (2017–18)

Early Life in Puerto Rico

MAD: *Everybody's interconnected. My parents married and had three kids, pretty much, you know, one, two, three. At that time, because of the economic situation in Puerto Rico, my father decided to come to the States to look for a job.*[37] *At that time, the only work there in rural Puerto Rico was working in the sugar cane fields, which was back-breaking, incredibly hard, hot work. It gets to be, you know, by eight o'clock in the morning, it's already eighty-five degrees in Puerto Rico, and you made five dollars a day being out there from sunup to sundown.*

MIRIAM ACEVEDO–DAVIS, INDIANA HISTORICAL SOCIETY

Miriam (right) with her sisters Iris Raquel (left) and Aida Enid, 1954

My mother's father got a job in the—working as a migrant worker in New Jersey and so recruited my father to join him. So he left us there in Puerto Rico and came up to New Jersey to work in the tomato fields as a migrant worker. Then after a year, he was able to send for us, and we moved over to Brooklyn, New York, where he was able to find a job at a factory. So, we lived in different neighborhoods there, usually near other families. And so, typical of immigrant families, we, you know, we clustered together. So, an uncle or an aunt or a cousin lived nearby and helped us get an apartment nearby. And so, we all lived pretty much near each other, and it also allowed us to keep our culture because of—you're all together, you're speaking the language and sharing food and holidays and that kind of stuff.

Above: Miriam Acevedo–Davis (right), her mother, Guadalupe (left), and her daughter Kamille, 2017; Left: Miriam Acevedo–Davis, executive director of La Plaza in Indianapolis, ca. 2013

Diversity of Childhood Neighborhood

MAD: *Yeah, other than remembering it being very diverse—we lived at—in a very diverse community. Our next-door neighbors were Jewish. The neighbors across the way were African American—just come up from the South. And so I remember, we all picked up Southern accents that summer (laughter). And we learned all about the different Jewish holidays. So, it was really interesting to be—to grow up in a really diverse community, as well as being very mired, very entrenched in our own culture. We only spoke Spanish at home, only ate, you know, Puerto Rican food. I remember as kids, we wanted spaghetti and meatballs because we would see it on television and our, you know, friends would have it. My mother tried to make it, and she didn't know how to make meatballs, so she took Vienna sausages and cut them up and put them in (laughter).*

Experiences with the Upward Bound Program

MAD: *Upward Bound—and all of a sudden, college was a real possibility, both in the sense that one had the (pauses) academic ability, but then it was also doable. Yeah, they took us to visit colleges—but also the cultural piece. They took us to plays and out to dinner and really exposed us to the whole city. We'd never—you know, we grew up in East New York and Brooklyn—which is actually this horrible ghetto, which we had no idea back then it was a terrible ghetto. We just thought it was home. And when they took us to a college for summer learning, we were astonished that, you know, communities in Brooklyn had grass and that there was a beach there. We were like, "Shut up?!" The only beach we knew about was Coney Island, and so we went through these neighborhoods that had lawns and big houses; and we just saw tenement houses where we grew up or small row houses. So, that was the start of—even just in Brooklyn itself—realizing there was a whole other world. Although we grew up in a very diverse community, economically, we didn't see a diverse community per se. And so being taken out like that, we were just astonished that in other parts of Brooklyn, people lived in houses that had, you know, a two-car garage and grass, and we were like. . . . And a backyard, we were like, "Shut up!" And a basement, "Oh my God!"*

NML: Such a luxury.

MAD: *It was luxuries that we knew nothing about, and what have you, and so that was really neat. But the program also really added a cultural piece so that we went to museums and, you know, all kinds of activities—plays. We saw every play on Broadway.*

Going to College during the Chicano Civil Rights Movement

MAD: *And then when [I] left there looking for jobs, the great thing is that, when I was in college, it was at the height of not only the Civil Rights Movement but the Women's Movement as well.*[38] *So it was—we were in college and in a women's college—things were changing as we lived there. For example, my freshman year, you were no longer required to wear skirts to dinner and to have a waited meal. You could just go through the line, and you could wear jeans and what have you. Before that, it was—you had to wear skirts to dinner and all of that. So, things were changing. You could wear pants and what have you. Careers were now opening, where in the past it was really, you know, the traditional careers for women. All of a sudden now people were talking about going to law school, medical school, you know, becoming chemical engineers and all of that. So, it was a really opportune time growing up because it was the Civil Rights Movement.*

And growing up in Brooklyn, we had the Young Lords that were talking about, you know, our civil rights, particularly for Latinos and demanding that we have equal rights and have the resources—the health and social services for families and what have you—but a real sense of ethnic pride as well.[39] *That—you know, being Latino was super-duper cool. Of course, the Chicano Movement on the West Coast was coming out as well.*[40] *When I got to college, there was a whole [student] chapter at Wesleyan University, just down the road from us—of Chicano students.*[41] *And so we would get together a couple of times a year to talk about our different cultures and to, you know, ask for more admissions for more Latinos and what have you. The Native American Movement was born on up at the Dartmouth—so met with the kids who were, you know, Native American up at Dartmouth and talking about Native American rights.*[42]

Latino Organizations in Indianapolis

MAD: *Up here, yeah. And actually, that's how I got involved with the Hispanic Education.*[43] *So, I actually wrote to the Hispanic Center and met with Mónica Medina there and talked to her about doing volunteer work there. And she said, "Let me see what we can do. I'll get back to you." And so, we always stayed in touch, and then I saw in the paper—Indianapolis Star—that their community was starting the Hispanic Education Center. So, I wrote to them and said, "I'm a graduate student. I'm up here two, three times a week. If you can use someone as a*

volunteer, please let me know." They called me immediately and put me on their board. . . .

There were probably half a dozen organizations. It was El Centro Hispano, *Fiesta Indianapolis, the Hispanic Education Center, the Hispanic Chamber of Latino—Hispanic Chamber of Commerce, there was SADCO [Sociedad Amigos de Columbia] and probably a Mexican civic group.*[44] *It might have been* Amigos á México—*I can't—there was a group, I can't remember now what name. And so maybe half a dozen organizations here in the city. I think more at the behest of funders, who said, you know, find a way to partner together and collaborate on that. And that had been a long way before I got in the picture of the organizations talking about how best to collaborate. In 2002* La Plaza *was formed to be the umbrella organization for those organizations.*[45] *Coincidentally, at that same time, the Community Centers of Indianapolis, which was an umbrella, was coming apart, and so the community shied away from an umbrella organization. Then that sent us back to the drawing board at that time. I was involved through the Hispanic Education Center, and we hired some consultants. There's nothing like being watched to make you behave yourself (laughs). At that point, the organizations agreed to a merger—a legal merger of those three organizations—it was El Centro Hispano, Hispanic Education Center, and Fiesta into* La Plaza, *which had been that umbrella organization. The Chamber of Commerce, as a 501(c)(6), which can do lobbying, was not allowed to merge by the IRS, because they had a different designation.*[46] *They spun off and became the Hispanic Business Council with the Greater Indianapolis Chamber. So instead, the three little organizations and* La Plaza *all merged together in 2004, 2005.*

Alfonso and Daniela Vidal

Alfonso and Daniela Vidal were both born in Caracas, Venezuela, in the early 1970s. Alfonso came to Evansville, Indiana, because it was considered safe and family lived there. The two were married in December 1997, and Daniela later joined Alfonso in Evansville. The couple has been active in business and organizing the Latino community in the area. These interview excerpts speak to the establishment and impact of an organization they founded for Latinos called Hospitality and Outreach for Latin America (HOLA).

Date of interview: November 16, 2017 | Ages at time of interview: Alfonso, 44; Daniela, 43 | Interview transcript audited by Nancy M. Germano (2017–18)

Establishing HOLA

DV: *Yeah, so when I was doing the MBA, I did some training for creative problem solving with Sue Ellspermann.[47] So she came in, and so I met—it was 1999—so I met her then, and then we, kind of, became good friends. She was my mentor, you know. She continues to be my mentor. And so, because I was trained as a facilitator with her, in 2001, Bishop [Gerald Andrew] Gettelfinger asked her to do a needs assessment of the Latino community in the 231 corridor—so, like Jasper, Huntingburg—because at that point, that's where really the majority of Latinos were in southern Indiana.[48] I mean, Evansville had like slim to none (laughs). But there was quite a strong community in that 231 highway, kind of corridor.*

So, she asked me to help her facilitate and be an—and interpret, you know, so that we could have this kind of Anglo and Latino groups together. So, we did that for a year. Like once a month, we would go there on a Saturday and have these listening sessions with the community and really identified—it was very eye-opening to me because again, our kind of immigration story is very different from many immigrants that were in that area—I mean, in the situations that we were. So it really, you know, helped me realize, you know, what a big need and struggle it was. Like I said, in Evansville there weren't that many, but soon afterwards, we really have an explosion of immigrants coming into Evansville. But it was a very helpful experience to have done that.

And then what the conclusion of that was is that, yeah, they had these kind of like their pastoral needs for the church—you know, the baptism and the—but they also had a very big, kind of, outreach material need of, you know, English, housing,

school, you know, all these other things. So that prompted the creation of the Guadalupe Center out of—in Huntingburg—that was really set up to address all those other needs that the community had.[49] And that helped us kind of see how that worked. So, when a year later the community started rapidly growing in Evansville, then it, kind of, prompted that.

AV: *We realized that there was a challenge, right? So, Maura Robinson invited us to a meeting in her house where the mayor—at the time was Russ Lloyd Jr.—was going to come and listen to our, you know, just a Q & A type session.[50] And what came out of that is that—it was Maura, Rodney Fonseca, Áldarez Camila, Daniela, and myself—we got together, and we said we need to do something about this, and we started HOLA.[51] HOLA is Hospitality and Outreach for Latin America, and that really has defined our lives. . . .*

DV: *We, kind of, talked about organizations we belong or serve in, so—but yeah, so that—I mean, really HOLA has always given us that opportunity to connect and engage and understand how things work in this country because, obviously, it's different, you know, very different from our country—and also provide that perspective as well, you know, saying, "Well here's why the community behaves this way," or "Here's why Latinos do certain things," because, you know, we bring that kind of cultural aspect to it—but really understand, kind of, the world of nonprofits and of government and now academia—now that I am at the university—and how it all interacts. And how can you effect true impactful change by understanding the system and then working within the system to drive that change. I think that was one of the key things that we've learned and become able to do, just because of that awareness. You know, versus maybe just go out and protest, you know, say, "Well, let's do things in a way that is going to really advance the conversation and provide results that are a win-win—that everybody feels is a win-win." I think to us that was important, and that's how we've always led HOLA—is that it has to be both communities coming together. It's never been about let's just keep the Latino community over here and give them everything. No, it's about let's truly come together as one community that's richer and that has, you know, both things that make them unique, make them even better.*

Daniela Vidal and Senator Richard Lugar at a Women in Leadership forum in Washington, DC, 2007

HOLA's Impact

NML: So, do you feel like with the formation of HOLA that that really helped increase the Latino population in Evansville? Because you said it was slim to none when you got here and now it's growing.

DV: *Yeah, well, I mean, I've said—*

AV: *No, I'd—*

DV: *It's not necessarily because of HOLA. Like, when we started HOLA, like that year—the last couple of years—there were a few businesses that started here, like, you know, distribution centers that brought a lot of Latino workforce. And then it quickly grew.*

AV: *Yeah, the population was prone to grow on itself.*

HOLA dance group in Evansville

DV: *So, what we did is we kind of got ahead of that and said—as we saw it growing—we kind of said, "Okay, let's help the city," because we kind of knew—preemptively—we said, "We know what's going to happen. If nothing—nobody does anything, it is going to explode—this population—and there's no—the city is not ready."*

I mean, the school system, which was 33,000 students, did not have one bilingual person in it! Not one, no ESL [English as a second language class], nothing. And they were getting—they were going to get bombarded with all these kids—because, actually, they were already seeing it, and they were like, "We are absolutely not prepared for this."

The police department was not prepared for it. And so, we were talking to them about, you know, if you stop a Latino—in our countries we're supposed to get out of the car. And so, if you stop a Latino, we're going to get out of the car. You are going to be yelling at them in English, "Stay in the car! Stay in the car!"

They're not going to understand what you are saying, and you are going to shoot them. So, things like that that just—

NML: The cultural nuances.

DV: *Yeah. So, we—*

AV: *So, we helped set the ground, okay—or prepare the ground—that when the Latino population would come, that we'd be there. For example, I was in the chamber of commerce*

for eleven years. Just now, we started a Latino Chamber Alliance.[52] Okay? But I was there the moment that it was key to start talking. As a board member on—when the other people wanted to start a separate Latino chamber of commerce, which made absolute no sense, you know? We would not have the resources to pay for a chamber of commerce, so, you know, the most logical thing would be to integrate it into the existing chamber of commerce. So, help all those—I mean everything—I mean, you think about economic development, the—politically—think about all those things, and then you have—so HOLA helped bridge that gap.

DV: *Yeah. So, in the very beginning, it's like I said—you know, like, the hospitals didn't have any bilingual resources and the school, the police, the city. So, we helped the mayor, and said, "Okay, how we can help?" And so all that established, kind of, some traveling city halls where we would provide translation. And so, that helped kind of, like I said, bridge that gap. We started doing a lot of health—like, monthly health clinics and health fairs. Then eventually, now all the hospitals have their own kind of Latino outreach person. So, the community needs have evolved to where—now HOLA is evolving as well. But initially, that was where the immediate needs were—like ESL classes and health, you know—because access to health was at a critical, urgent need. So, we were there to provide that.*

Lupe "Lu" Figueroa, daughter of Consuelo and Francisco Figueroa, was raised in East Chicago, where she worked in the judicial system. She is pictured here at a swearing-in ceremony during the 1960s.

Conclusion

Capturing Hoosier Latino History: A Beginning

Latinos have been called many things throughout the history of the United States. They have been known as Hispanic, Chicano, Latino, and now Latinx. While their designation has changed, this group of people, united by shared culture and history, has endured the seizure of their lands in what is now the American Southwest, brutal violence, denial of citizenship, discrimination, racism, and expulsion. Despite all this, they have worked hard to help build this nation, including the State of Indiana. In fact, Latinos were part of this nation before its inception, as they settled in what is now the American Southwest before the landing of the *Mayflower*. Since then, they have contributed to the American Revolution and every war that followed. Today, many of them serve in the military, politics, business and nonprofits, education, the arts, and in many other fields.

As this book has shown, Indiana Latinos are a centennial community with generations of history in the state. Hoosier Latinos established vibrant *barrios*. They developed cultural and religious institutions that persist today, such as the *Fiestas Patrias* parade and Our Lady of Guadalupe Catholic Church in Indiana Harbor. At the same time, they helped build the industrial powerhouse that Northwest Indiana became in the early-twentieth century by working in steel mills such as Inland Steel and U.S. Steel. Despite setbacks, especially the devastating expulsion of Mexicans and Mexican Americans that took place in Indiana and around the nation in the early-1930s, Latinos persisted. They established lasting businesses, such as *El Popular*, which still operates today, the newspaper *Latin Times* that spoke to Hoosier Latino issues, and ran and eventually won political offices, and so much more.

As the twentieth century advanced, and a more diverse Latino population arrived in the state, new communities were established in larger cities such as Indianapolis, but also in smaller cities and towns. Organizations such as the *El Centro* Hispano–American Multi Service Center began to spring up in the state to help new Latino immigrants. Meanwhile, Hoosier Latina Carmen Velásquez helped migrant farmworkers in Grant County, gaining the support of both the Catholic Church and a farmworker advocacy organization called AMOS (Associated Migrant Opportunity Services).

During the 1970s and 1980s, Latinos made themselves more visible and started exerting influence. They began entering the political arena, following individuals such as Jesse Gómez, who was elected to the East Chicago City Council in 1963, making him one of the first Hoosier Latino politicians. Hoosier Latinos also founded cultural institutions, such as the Phoenix Theatre, co-created by Bryan Fonseca in 1983. Others took up leadership positions in Indiana's education system. For example, Greg Chávez championed bilingual education in the South Bend schools, beginning in the 1980s.

The contributions of Latinos in the last few decades have accelerated as the Latino population has ballooned. Population growth is driven not just by continued emigration from Latin America, but also by the migration of Latin Americans across the United States and the births of new generations of Latinos in the United States. As their population has grown in Indiana, some Latinos have stepped in to help new immigrants acclimate to their new homes and surrounding culture. In 2002 Alfonso and Daniela Vidal, together with other community members, cofounded an immigrant support organization in Evansville, Indiana. Named HOLA (Hospitality and Outreach for Latin America), it not only provides support and information about living in a new place, but it also celebrates the diversity among Evansville's growing Latino population.

Latinos are so many things in Indiana: professionals, business leaders, and entrepreneurs who create jobs and cultural vibrancy. Migrant farmworkers fill our tables with sustenance, educators strive to make sure that none are left behind, and activists demand dignity and a voice for all at the table of governance. This book is dedicated to exploring that history, which has often been overlooked in the narrative of this country and state. Latino journalist and historian, Juan Gonzalez, explores this in his book *Harvest of Empire*, stating, "Once you admit Mexican's long history on U.S. soil, you must necessarily accept Hispanic culture and the Spanish language as integral components of our own national saga."[1]

This book is also dedicated to the strangely revolutionary idea that we should tell a fuller story of American history. Through the history and individual stories within *Hoosier Latinos: A Century of Struggle, Service, and Success*, people in Indiana, young and old, descendants of Latino American pioneers, Latino immigrants and their descendants, those who have Latino friends and colleagues, and those who have no connection to these communities, will hopefully come to understand that Latino culture and history are foundational in the United States and have transformed the Hoosier State in important ways. This history *matters*—not as a side note to the nation or state's history—but as an integral part of it. It is important not just to honor those who deserve credit for their contributions, but also because erasing people's history is a key component of "othering." As anthropologist Sujey Vega explains in her book, *Latino Heartland*, "Forgetting details of marginalized communities suppresses their contributions and promotes even further silences. Harnessing the power to silence controls the narrative and determines how subsequent tales can be spun to maintain privilege."[2] This erasure turns the censored groups into "others," who are alien to those in the American mainstream rather than individuals who are already part of America. This fosters bias and fear, striking a dagger into the heart of American society by driving a wedge between neighbors. Re-envisioning historical narratives to include communities of all backgrounds cannot solve bias, but it can play an important role in the solution.

The process of re-examining long-held assumptions about where Latino stories can be found, and when they should be told, is one that requires investment and commitment on the part of community members and institutions. For its part, the Indiana Historical Society, itself dating back to 1830, has been part of that erasure of Latinos by failing to fully collect and preserve their stories and contributions. Recognizing this failure, in 2016 the IHS's staff and leaders began taking this task seriously by launching the Indiana Latino Collecting Initiative. Staff members began reaching out to Hoosier Latino communities and individuals, who for so long had been keeping their own histories and institutional memories. Under the leadership of Nicole Martinez–LeGrand, the IHS embarked on an ambitious project of conducting oral histories, researching historical and genealogical material for background, gathering and digitizing photos, and accessioning new materials into the Society's collections. The accessions include copies of Indiana's founding Latino newspaper, *El Amigo del Hogar,* a ledger book from Our Lady of Guadalupe—an early Latino Catholic Church—and photographs from a political march by farmworkers and supporters demanding rights and recognition. These are just a few of the vitally important materials that have been gathered as part of this initiative.

In 2018 the IHS hosted an exhibition of the materials and stories that staff had gathered called *Be Heard: Latino Experiences in Indiana*. It was the first effort by the Society to articulate a synthesis of the Latino contribution to the state. That exhibition has provided the foundation for this book, which is far from complete. My coauthor for the exhibit and this book, Nicole Martinez–LeGrand, and I recognize that the experience of a single individual cannot define the collective experience of many. But it can add insight into what it is like to uproot oneself, travel to a new land, plant new roots, and become part of a growing community. The IHS's Indiana Latino Collecting Initiative, this book included, is the start of a conversation with the statewide Latino community. More work is needed, including more families digging into and sharing their stories, and more cities and towns discovering and acknowledging the Latino heritage in their backyard.

Hoosier Latinos offers a glimpse into Latino Hoosier history that spans more than one hundred years. The history, photos, and interviews shared here are of individuals of varying cultural backgrounds who recall what it has been like to be Latino in the Hoosier State throughout the twentieth and early twenty-first centuries. This book by the Indiana Historical Society is just the start of an ongoing dialogue with the entire Hoosier community—to share Hoosier Latino history—and to convey the importance of weaving Latino history into the state's broader historical narrative.

Daniel Gonzales
Director, Exhibitions Research
Indiana Historical Society, Indianapolis
March 2021

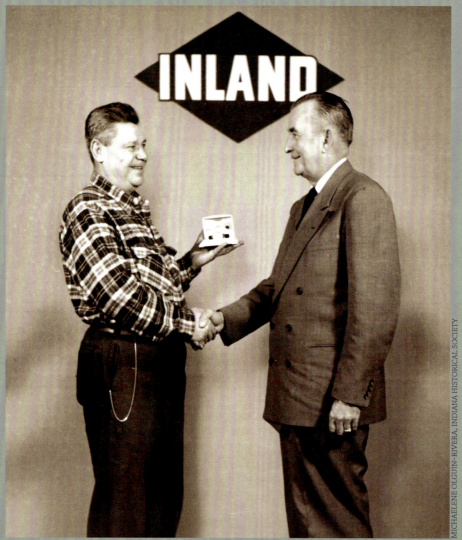

Antonio Medina receiving a retirement watch from an official at Inland Steel Company in East Chicago in 1959

Notes by Chapter

Introduction: Indiana Historical Society Initiative Addresses Neglect of Hoosier Latino History

1. "Becoming Part of the United States," Immigration and Relocation in U.S. History, Mexican, Library of Congress, https://www.loc.gov/classroom-materials/immigration/mexican/becoming-part-of-the-united-states/, accessed February 8, 2021.

2. "Town Brevities," *Noblesville Ledger* (Noblesville, IN), June 8, 1877; June 22, 1877.

3. "Personal Ads," *Indianapolis News*, June 17, 1878.

4. "One Hundred Mexicans Live in Indianapolis," *Indianapolis News*, June 23, 1919.

5. Department of Commerce–Bureau of the Census, Census of the United States: 1920-Population, Enumeration District 176, Page 6A, January 15, 1920, Ancestry.

Chapter 1
Founding of a Community, 1919–1929

1. Gilberto Cárdenas, "United States Immigration Policy toward Mexico: An Historical Perspective," *Chicana/o Latina/o Law Review*, 2 (1975), UCLA, https://escholarship.org/uc/item/0fh8773n, accessed September 22, 2021; "The Immigration Act of 1917," in The History of the Border, 1894 to Present Day, Texas-México Center blog, November 16, 2020, Southern Methodist University, Dallas, TX, https://blog.smu.edu/texasmexico/, accessed September 22, 2021; Gabriela F. Arredondo and Derek Vaillant, "Mexicans," 2004/2005, in *Electronic Encyclopedia of Chicago*, Chicago Historical Society/ Encyclopedia of Chicago, Newberry Library, http://www.encyclopedia.chicagohistory.org/pages/824.html, accessed September 22, 2021.

2. Paul Schuster Taylor, *Mexican Labor in the United States: Chicago and the Calumet Region*, vol. 2, no. 7 (Berkley, CA: University of California Press, 1932), 67.

3. Ibid., Table S, 49.

4. Francisco Arurto Rosales and Daniel T. Simon, "Mexican Immigrant Experience in the Urban Midwest: East Chicago, Indiana, 1919–1945," *Indiana Magazine of History* 77, no. 4 (December 1981): 333–57; repr. in *Forging a Community: The Latino Experience in Northwest Indiana, 1919–1975*, eds. Edward J. Escobar and James B. Lane, vol. 2 (Chicago, IL: Cattails Press, 1987).

5. Chelsea Sutton, "Meeting Fred Maravilla," Indiana Historical Society blog, November 2, 2018, https://indianahistory.org/blog/meeting-fred-maravilla/, accessed September 22, 2021.

6. Miguel A. Agurto, 1919, U.S. Panama Canal Zone, Employment Records and Sailing Lists, 1884–1937, Container 44, Ancestry.

7. Nicole Martinez–LeGrand, "Not all Latinos are Mexican: The Story of a 1920s Peruvian Steel Worker from Gary, Indiana," Indiana Historical Society blog, n.d., https://indianahistory.org/blog/not-all-latinos-are-mexican-the-story-of-a-1920s-peruvian-steel-worker-from-gary-indiana/, accessed September 22, 2021.

8. Rosales and Simon, "Mexican Immigrant Experience in the Urban Midwest," in *Forging a Community*, 152.

9. Taylor, *Mexican Labor in the United States*, vol. 2, no. 7, Table 23, 168.

10. Ibid.

11. Ibid., 133.

12. Rosales and Simon, "Mexican Immigrant Experience in the Urban Midwest," in *Forging a Community*, 142; Zaragosa Vargas, *Proletarians of the North: A History of Mexican Industrial Workers in Detroit and the Midwest, 1917–1933* (Oakland: University of California Press, 1999), 151.

13. Taylor, *Mexican Labor in the United States*, vol. 2, no. 7, 133.

14. "Mexicans Celebrate," *Hammond Times* (Hammond, IN), September 17, 1924.

15. "Closes with Parade," *Hammond Times*, September 17, 1926.

16. Phil Lamar Anderson, "Young Priest Builds $35,000 Church for Region's Mexicans," *Hammond Times*, July 19, 1940.

17. *Mexican American Harbor Lights: Pictorial History* (Indiana Harbor, East Chicago, IN: Señoras of Yesteryear, 1992), 36.

18. Anderson, "Young Priest Builds $35,000 Church for Region's Mexicans."

19. Abel Maravilla was too young to work in the steel mill. The other brothers worked at Inland Steel Company (1893–1998), which was acquired by Ispat International, which later became part of ArcelorMittal. "Our History," ArcelorMittal, accessed February 9, 2021. Abel later went west and settled in Nampa, Idaho.

20. After World War I, local unions around America tried and failed to strike for better working conditions. When these attempts failed, the American Federation of Labor and the Amalgamated Association of Iron, Steel, and Tin Workers called for a national strike of steelworkers. The Steel Strike of 1919, which also failed, lasted from September 21, 1919, to January 8, 1920. See Erin Blakemore, "Why the Great Steel Strike of 1919 Was One of Labor's Biggest Failures," September 23, 2019, in This Day in History, History.com, accessed February 8, 2021.

21. International Workers of the World (Wobblies) started in Chicago in 1905. They had perceived ties to socialist and anarchist movements. They believed all unions should be united into industrial unions. See "IWW History Project: Industrial Workers of the World, 1905–1935," in Civil Rights and Labor History Consortium, part of *Mapping American Social Movements through the Twentieth Century*, University of Washington, Seattle, https://depts.washington.edu/iww/, accessed February 10, 2021.

22. "Scab" is a term used for a non-union employee, particularly when that individual continues working during a labor strike. Persons who cross through picket lines in order to work are often called scabs.

23. The Maravilla family arrived in the United States on May 19, 1922, in Laredo, Texas, per a U.S. Department of Labor Immigration Service border crossing record. "U.S. Border Crossings from Mexico to U.S., 1895–1964, A3437 Laredo, Texas, 1903–1955," NARA Roll No. 076, Manifest, U.S. Department of Labor, Immigration Services, Mexican Border District, Serial No. 5299, Digital Image s.v. "Ignacio Maravilla," Ancestry.

24. Travelers Aid programs began in 1851 in Saint Louis, Missouri, to help those traveling to the West. In later years, these programs welcomed immigrants at many ports of entry. The programs' purpose is to ensure that newcomers are properly informed and have a place to stay and to assist stranded passengers. In the 1920s they operated most often in major railroad stations. See "America's Oldest Social Welfare Movement," Travelers Aid International, https://www.travelersaid.org/about-us/history/, accessed February 10, 2021.

25. Antonio Gordiano Medina was born in Comanja de Corona, Jalisco, Mexico, in May 1893. Antonio immigrated to the Indiana Harbor area from Mexico in 1916 per Border Crossing Nonstatistical Manifest, Laredo, Texas, Serial No. 13732, May 3, 1925, U.S., Border Crossing from Mexico to U.S, 1895–1964, A3437 Laredo, Texas, 1903–55," NARA Roll No. 93, Manifest, U.S. Department of Labor, Immigration Services, Serial No. 13732, Digital Image s.v. "Antonio Medina," Ancestry.

26. María de Jesús Reyes was born in Paso de Cuarenta, Jalisco, Mexico, in October 1906. She immigrated to the United States with her family on July 6, 1922, per Application for Resident Alien's Border Crossing Identification Card No. 5900, March 23, 1950, "U.S. Border Crossings from Mexico to U.S., 1895–1964," NARA Roll 118, Resident Alien's Border Crossing Identification Card, Digital Image s.v. "Maria Jesus Medina," Ancestry.

27. Antonio Medina and María de Jesús Reyes obtained their marriage license on December 20, 1926, at the Lake County, Indiana, Clerk Office, and were married on January 8, 1927, by Father Octavio Zavatta, per Lake County Clerk Office, State of Indiana, License No. 89606, Application Record 269, 1926–27, Volume 62.

28. During the Mexican Revolution (1910–20), a new national constitution was drafted in 1917. The new constitution greatly restricted the Roman Catholic Church in Mexico and its contributions to the State. Clergy were strictly prohibited from public displays and celebrations of faith. Prosecutions and violence against clergy occurred. President Plutarco Calles (1924–28) strongly enforced the constitution, resulting in the Cristero War (1926–29). See Consuelo S. Moreno, "The Movement that Sinned Twice: The Cristero War and Mexican Collective Memory," *History in the Making* 13, no. 1 (2020): 3, 4, https://scholarworks.lib.csusb.edu/history-in-the-making/vol13/iss1/5, accessed February 10, 2021.

29. On the 1940 census, the Medinas' neighbors' places of birth are given as primarily from Mexico, Romania, Hungary, Bulgaria, Yugoslavia, and Greece, along with other U.S. states. 1940 U.S. census, Lake County, East Chicago, Indiana, Ward 6, Block No. 76, Sheet 8B, Ancestry.

30. "Our History," ArcelorMittal." Youngstown Sheet and Tube (1923–77), founded in Ohio, had a plant in East Chicago, Indiana, from 1923 through the 1970s when it was acquired by Lykes Industries. See "Youngstown Sheet and Tube Co.," *Encyclopedia of Chicago*, http://www.encyclopedia.chicagohistory.org/pages/2913.html, accessed February 10, 2021.

31. *Comadre* in Spanish means "co-mother" in reference to a mother's child being the godchild of another person. For a man it is *compadre*, or "co-father." The plural tense for a couple is *compadres*, or "co-parents." It is also a traditional term of reverence for a close and dear friendship. See *Merriam–Webster* online.

32. *Pozole* or *posole* is a Mexican-style traditional soup, which translates to the English word "hominy." The soup is made with pork or chicken, spices, and hominy, garnished with shredded cabbage, chile peppers, onion, radishes, cilantro, and avocado. This dish is traditionally made for special holidays or family celebrations. *Menudo* is a spicy soup made from tripe.

33. José Anguiano (1901–1989) was a member of the *Sociedad Mexicana Cuauhtémoc*.

34. Each social group nominated a candidate to be the annual *Fiestas Patrias* queen.

35. A *chambelán* is an official escort, or man of honor, to the *Fiestas Patrias* queen.

36. "Frederico" was later identified as Conrado Calderón (life dates unknown), who was the queen's *chambelán*.

37. Benjamín Figueroa and his family lived in the same building as his brother Francisco. 1930 U.S. Census, East Chicago, Lake County, Indiana, page 6A, Enumeration District 0120, FHL microfilm 2340336, Ancestry.

38. On the 1940 U.S. census, the Garza family lived in the same building as the Figueroa family at 3509 Deodar Street. 1940 U.S. Census, East Chicago, Lake County, Indiana, Roll m-t0627-01065, page 6A, Enumeration District 45–32, Ancestry.

Chapter 2
Era of Tumultuous Growth, 1929–1969

1. "Mexican Resentful over Alleged Police Injustice," *Whiting Evening Times* (Whiting, IN), August 25, 1931; Francisco Arurto Rosales and Daniel T. Simon, "Mexican Immigrant Experience in the Urban Midwest: East Chicago, Indiana, 1919–1945," *Indiana Magazine of History* 77, no. 4 (December 1981): 333–57; repr., in *Forging a Community: The Latino Experience in Northwest Indiana, 1919–1975*, eds. Edward J. Escobar and James B. Lane, vol. 2 (Chicago, IL: Cattails Press, 1987). "The Wickersham Commission is the popular name for the National Commission on Law Observance and Enforcement, which was appointed by President Herbert Hoover in 1929. The commission . . . conducted the first comprehensive national study of crime and law enforcement in U.S. history," covering "every aspect of the criminal justice system, including the causes of crime, police and prosecutorial procedures, and the importance of probation and parole." From "Wickersham Commission," https://law.jrank.org/pages/11309/Wickersham-Commission.html, accessed February 12, 2021.

2. Elizabeth N. Wilson, "Notes on the Early History of the International Institute of Gary," *International Institute Papers*, Calumet Regional Archives (September 1932).

3. Raymond A. Mohl and Neil Betten, "Discrimination and Repatriation: Mexican Life in Gary," in *Forging a Community: The Latino Experience in Northwest Indiana, 1919–1975*, eds. Edward J. Escobar and James B. Lane, vol. 2 (Chicago, IL: Cattails Press, 1987), 164–73.

4. "The Story of Unemployment Relief Work in Lake County, Indiana," December 31, 1932, Lake County Relief Committee and Indiana Commission for Relief and Distress Due to Unemployment, cover page summary, Hammond Public Library.

5. "Colony Here Reduced to Low Figure: Only 3,500 Mexicans Left in Twin City after Big Exodus," *Twin City News* (East Chicago/Indiana Harbor, IN), July 26, 1932.

6. Paul Schuster Taylor, *Mexican Labor in the United States: Chicago and the Calumet Region*, vol. 2, no. 7 ([Berkeley]: University of California Press, 1932), Table 12, 55.

7. "Story of Unemployment Relief Work in Lake County," 11.

8. John Fraire, "Mexicans Playing Baseball in Indiana Harbor, 1925–1942," *Indiana Magazine of History* 110, no. 2 (2014): 127.

9. Jill Weiss Simins, "Braceros in the Corn Belt, Part Two: 'Ambassadors of Good Will,'" Indiana Historical Bureau blog, March 13, 2019, https://blog.history.in.gov/tag/bracero-program/, accessed February 19, 2021.

10. "Mexican Farm Labor Treated Worse than Prisoners of War," September 24, 1954, Newspaper clippings from Archive of the Archdiocese of Saint Louis, RG07816.

11. Simins, "Braceros in the Corn Belt, Part Two."

12. Ibid.

13. "Heinz Company Leases 300 Acre Eely Est. Farm: Mexican Labor to Be Used to Harvest Crops," *Argos Reflector* (Argos, IN), May 4, 1933.

14. Lorena Oropeza, "Latinos in World War II: Fighting on Two Fronts," National Park Service, https://www.nps.gov/articles/latinoww2.htm, accessed February 19, 2021.

15. Frederick Ruiz Maravilla Oral History Interview, 2016, Indiana Latino History Project, SC 3355, Indiana Historical Society; Maurer Maurer, *Air Force Combat Units of World War II* (Washington DC: Office of Air Force History, 1983), 324–25.

16. "Corps Fete WAC," *Hammond Times* (Hammond, IN), June 29, 1944.

17. Edwin Maldonado, "Contract Labor and the Origins of Puerto Rican Communities in the United States," in *Forging a Community: The Latino Experience in Northwest Indiana, 1919–1975*, eds. Edward J. Escobar and James B. Lane, vol. 2 (Chicago, IL: Cattails Press, 1987), 206.

18. Edward Medina Oral History Interview, 2016, 2017, Indiana Latino History Project, SC 3387, Indiana Historical Society.

19. "All for One and One for All," About Us, League of United Latin American Citizens, https://lulac.org/about/, accessed February 19, 2021.

20. Rosemarie Gómez Oral History Interview, 2018, Indiana Latino History Project, Indiana Historical Society.

21. Dale Burgess, "Here's Migrant Worker Situation in Indiana," *Rushville Republican* (Rushville, IN), August 6, 1970.

22. "Migrant Grantees Directory: Title III-B Programs and Key Staff," National Migrant Information Clearinghouse, Juárez–Lincoln Center, August 1973, https://files.eric.ed.gov/fulltext/ED081541.pdf, accessed February 20, 2021; Children of María Carmen Velásquez Oral History Interview, 2017, Indiana Latino History Project, SC 3478, Indiana Historical Society.

23. Anthony Seed, "Migrant Aid Office Here," *Republic* (Columbus, IN), December 28, 1974.

24. Simins, "Braceros in the Corn Belt, Part Two."

25. Inga Kim, "The 1965–1970 Delano Grape Strike and Boycott," United Farm Workers blog, March 7, 2017, https://ufw.org/1965-1970-delano-grape-strike-boycott/, accessed February 19, 2021.

26. Title VII—Bilingual Education Programs, Pub. L. No. 90-247, 81 Stat. 816 (1968).

27. Taylor, *Mexican Labor in the United States*, vol. 2, no. 7, 67.

28. Rosales and Simon, "Mexican Immigrant Experience in the Urban Midwest," in *Forging a Community*, 143.

29. Sister Mary Helen Rogers, "The Role of Our Lady of Guadalupe Parish in the Adjustment of the Mexican Community to Life in the Indiana Harbor Area," in *Forging a Community: The Latino Experience in Northwest Indiana, 1919–1975*, eds. Edward J. Escobar and James B. Lane, vol. 2 (Chicago, IL: Cattails Press, 1987), 199.

30. "Housing Ordinance Passed in Twin City," *Hammond Times*, October 14, 1959.

31. Ibid.

32. James Shannon, "Twin City Fund Aid Clipped," *Hammond Times*, February 12, 1965.

33. "Purdue Foundation Stays," *Hammond Times*, March 26, 1969.

34. "One Hundred Mexicans Live in Indianapolis," *Indianapolis News* (Indianapolis, IN), June 23, 1916.

35. Charles C. Guthrie, "Hispanic Indianapolis: Personal Histories from an Emerging Community," Oral History Project, 1990, BV 3523, Indiana Historical Society.

36. "Mexican Families Came from Texas," *Indianapolis News*, October 14, 1977; 1930 U.S. Census, Indianapolis, Indiana, Sheet 3A, Ancestry.

37. Taylor, *Mexican Labor in the United States*, vol. 2, no. 7, 28, 63–68.

38. "Mexicano Club Elects Officers," *Indianapolis Star*, June 9, 1958.

39. Mexican repatriation, or the Repatriation Movement, lasted from 1929 to 1936. This was a mandate that was carried out by American authorities to return Mexican nationals back to Mexico. It affected many Mexican families with U.S.-born children. Many returned voluntarily due to the economic depression and the lack of employment and social relief aid. The Immigration and Naturalization Service (INS) cooperated with local governments that sought to remove Mexicans from their jurisdiction. At the time, social relief agencies began to feel pressure to exclude foreign-born applicants from receiving aid. Other local governments used the threat of federal immigration law—by which immigrants who became "public charges" could be deported—as a way to discourage them from requesting aid. INS maintains that it was not the organization that instituted the removal protocol. Rosales and Simon, "Mexican Immigrant Experience in the Urban Midwest" in *Forging a Community*, 146–47.

40. The SS *Normandie* was a French ocean liner owned by the *Compagnie Générale Transatlantique*. When it debuted in 1935, it was noted as the largest and fastest passenger ship due to its turbo-electric propulsion. This ship made 139 transatlantic trips from France to New York. In 1942 it was seized by U.S. authorities and renamed the USS *Lafayette*. It caught fire during its refurbishing and capsized in 1942 while in New York and was scrapped in 1946. "*Queen Mary, Mauretania* to Become Troop Ships," *Hammond Times*, March 20, 1940.

41. By the summer of 1943 the United States had eliminated the Axis Powers in North Africa. Naples is a port city on Italy's western coast. Foggia, located on the opposite side of Italy, northeast of Naples, was occupied by the U.S. Army in late-1943. The Naples–Foggia Campaign lasted from September 9, 1943, to January 21, 1944. Col. Kenneth V. Smith, "Naples–Foggia, 1943–44," U.S. Army Center of Military History, https://history.army.mil/brochures /naples/72-17.htm, accessed August 3, 2021.

42. The Rome–Arno Campaign lasted from January to September 1944. Clayton D. Laurie, "Rome–Arno, 1944," U.S. Army Center of Military History, https://history.army.mil/brochures/romar/72-20 .htm, accessed March 1, 2021.

43. Albert Kesselring was a German *luftwaffe* [air force] field marshal during World War II. He was the German commander in the Mediterranean Theater and for some military operations in North Africa. In addition to his military accomplishments, he was known for massacres committed by troops under his command in Italy. After the war, he was tried and sentenced to death for his war crimes but was released in 1952 due to his health. "Albert Kesselring," *Encyclopedia Britannica*, https://www.britannica.com/.

44. The 450th Bombardment Group and its subordinate squadrons (720th, 721st, 722nd, and 723rd) received credit for the following battles: Air Offensive Europe (July 4, 1942–June 5, 1944), Naples–Foggia (August 10, 1943–January 21, 1944), Air Combat Balkans (November 1, 1943–December 31, 1944), Rome–Arno (January 22–September 9, 1944), Po Valley (April 5–May 8, 1944), Normandy (June 6, 1944–July 24, 1945), Northern France (July 25–September 14, 1944), Southern France (August 15–September 9, 1944), Northern Apennines (September 10, 1944–April 4, 1945), and Rhineland (September 15, 1944–March 21, 1945). Maurer, *Air Force Combat Units of World War II*, 324–25.

45. The country of Italy is shaped like a boot.

46. Many African countries were in France's possession during World War II, including the modern day nations of: Morocco, Tunisia (until 1956); Guinea (until 1958); Cameroon, Central African Republic (formerly Oubangui–Chari), Chad, Gabon, Ivory Coast, Madagascar, Mali (formerly Sudan), Nigeria, Republic of Congo, Togo (formerly Togoland) (until 1960); Algeria (until 1962), Djibouti (formerly Somaliland) (until 1977), as well as several islands. See "Timeline: French Empire, c. 1630–1977," online version, History World, 2012, Oxford Reference, Oxford University Press, https://www.oxford reference.com/, accessed June 28, 2021.

47. The Tuskegee Airmen was an African American military pilot group with the U.S. Army Air Forces, based and trained in Tuskegee, Alabama. They formed the 332nd Fighter Group in July 1942, serving first with the Twelfth Air Force flying P-40s and P-39s. They were later moved to the Fifteenth Air Force, where they escorted B-17 and B-24 heavy bombers on campaigns over Italy and southern Europe with P-39s and P-47s. After this they flew P-51s, the "brand-new planes" that Fred Maravilla described in his interview. A second detachment of Tuskegee flyers formed the 477th Bombardment Group, although they were never deployed overseas. Maurer, *Air Force Combat Units of World War II*, 212–13, 349–50; Maurer Maurer, *Combat Squadrons of the Air Force—World War II* (Washington DC: Office of Air Force History, 1982), 329–30; "The Tuskegee Airmen: The African American Pilots of World War II," The National WWII Museum, https://www.nationalww2museum.org/sites/default/files/2017-07 /tuskegee-airmen.pdf, accessed March 1, 2021.

48. The Mariana Islands Campaign, known as Operation Forager, occurred between June and November 1944. It affected the islands of Mariana and Palau. "The Marianas Campaign," National Museum of the U.S. Navy, Naval History and Heritage Command, https://www .history.navy.mil/, accessed June 29, 2021.

49. Catechist Missionary Society was located at 3869 Block Avenue in East Chicago.

50. The original transcripts are not altered. However, when an interviewee reviews the transcript of his or her interview and changes a word or phrase, the original word/phrase in the transcript is lined through and the correct word or phrase is placed in brackets.

51. Bremerhaven is a port city located in northern Germany on the North Sea. It is seventy-six miles west of Hamburg. During World War II, this was a strategic location for the Nazi War navy. It was a location with multiple shipyards, an aircraft factory, an oil refinery, a steel mill, and protective shelters for German U-boats. In April 1945 it was bombed and captured by the British Royal Air Force and the U.S. Eighth Air Force. Bremerhaven was also the location of two concentration camps, Bremen–Farge and Bremen–Vegesack. The harbor in Bremerhaven was used by Allied forces to provide supplies after the war. The base was called Carl Schurz Kaserne and was run by both U.S. and British military. In 1993 the U.S. army vacated the base. "Bremerhaven," *Encyclopedia Britannica*.

52. Zweibrücken, which means "two bridges," is located in western Germany, about seventeen miles from the French border. During World War II, this town was located in the "red zone" along the heavily fortified Westwall, or *Siegfried* line. This was the line that the Allies needed to breach in order to invade Germany at the end of the war, which they did during the Rhineland campaign. The town of Zweibrücken was evacuated in 1939–40. After the war it became a part of the Rhineland–Palatinate state. Ted Ballard, "Rhineland," U.S. Army

Office of Military History, https://history.army.mil/brochures/rhineland/rhineland.htm, accessed April 15, 2021.

53. After World War II, Germany was divided into two zones. West Germany was jointly governed by Britain, France, and the United States, while the Soviet Union claimed East Germany. Although Berlin was located in East Germany, the city itself was split in half, separated by the Berlin Wall. "The Cold War in Berlin," John F. Kennedy Presidential Library and Museum, https://www.jfklibrary.org/, accessed April 15, 2021.

54. West Point, also known as the United States Military Academy, was established in 1802 under the directive of President Thomas Jefferson. Today it is a four-year, coeducational federal service academy in West Point, Orange County, New York. Many graduates enter the army, usually at the rank of second lieutenant. "United States Military Academy," *Encyclopedia Britannica*; "A Brief History of West Point," United States Military Academy, https://www.westpoint.edu/about/history-of-west-point, accessed September 22, 2021.

55. The Cudahy Packing Company was a meat packing firm that was first located in Wisconsin in the late 1800s. By 1922 it had expanded to ten U.S. cities, including East Chicago, Indiana. The company, which specialized in sliced dried beef, sliced bacon, and Italian-style sausage, was purchased by General Host in 1968 and dissolved in the 1970s. "Cudahy Packing Co.," *Encyclopedia of Chicago*, http://www.encyclopedia.chicagohistory.org/pages/2635.html, accessed March 1, 2021.

56. The economic downturn in the industrialized world known as the Great Depression began with the stock market crash of October 1929. "Great Depression," *Encyclopedia Britannica*.

57. Cantinflas was the stage name of Mario Fortino Alfonso Moreno Reyes (1911–1993), a Mexican comic film actor, producer, and screenwriter as well as an iconic figure in Mexico and Latin America. Jorge Alberto Negrete Moreno (1911–1953) was a Mexican singer and actor. "Cantinflas," *Encyclopedia Britannica*.

58. The Indiana Theatre opened in 1925 at 3548 Michigan Avenue in East Chicago, Indiana, and closed in 1973. The Garden Theatre opened in 1918 as a silent movie house at 3424 Main Street in East Chicago and was demolished after the city declared it structurally unsafe in 2001. "Curtains for Garden Theater," *Hammond Times*, February 15, 2001; "Indiana Theatre," Cinema Treasures, http://cinematreasures.org/theaters/15412, accessed March 1, 2021.

59. John F. Kennedy (1917–1963) served as U.S. president from 1961 to 1963. Richard M. Nixon (1913–1994) served as vice president from 1953 to 1961 and ran unsuccessfully against Kennedy in the 1960 presidential campaign. "Life of John F. Kennedy," John F. Kennedy Library and Museum, https://www.jfklibrary.org/, accessed March 1, 2021; "Richard M. Nixon," The White House, https://www.whitehouse.gov/, accessed March 1, 2021.

60. John B. Nicosia (1910–1985) served as mayor of East Chicago from 1964 to 1971. Robert A. Pastrick (1927–2016) served as mayor of East Chicago from 1972 to 2004. Walter M. Jeorse (1909–1983) served as mayor of East Chicago from 1952 to 1963. Lu Ann Franklin, "Thirteen Men Have Led the City on Its Course," *Times of Northwest Indiana* (Munster, IN), February 23, 1993; Jim Masters, "Pabey New E. C. Mayor," *Times of Northwest Indiana*, December 29, 2004.

61. Victor Manuel Martínez (1928–2008), Social Security Death Index, Indiana, Social Security Death Index Master File, Social Security Administration, Ancestry.

62. Jesse Gómez (1920–1979) was elected East Chicago, Indiana, city councilman in 1963, the first Hispanic (of Mexican heritage) to hold a seat on the East Chicago city council. "Councilman 6th District," *Hammond Times*, May 5, 1963.

63. See Edward Medina interview excerpts at the end of Chapters 1 and 2 in this book.

64. A *sombrero* is a traditional Mexican straw hat with a high, pointed crown and a wide brim. *Maracas* are Latin and Caribbean musical percussion instruments often made of hollowed gourds with pebbles or beans inside and a handle attached for shaking. "Sombrero" and "Maraca" in *Encyclopedia Britannica*.

65. The Third Order Society of Saint Francis is an Anglican/Franciscan religious order, founded by Saint Francis for both lay and ordained people who live by Franciscan principles "in the world," serving God in their ordinary occupations of life. The Third Order was established by Saint Francis himself in the early-thirteenth century, however a chapter wasn't founded in the United States until 1917. "About the Third Order" and "What is the Third Order?" The Third Order, Society of St. Francis, Province of the Americas, https://tssf.org/, accessed April 1, 2021.

66. The parish of Saint Paul Catholic Church, which began in 1868 in a frame structure at Ninth and Branson Streets, dedicated a new brick Gothic structure on Branson Street in 1897, built a new church in 1977 and relocated it to its present location at 1031 Kem Road, Marion, Indiana. "Parish History," St. Paul Catholic Church and School, https://stpaulcatholicmarion.com/parish-history, accessed March 1, 2021.

67. Saint Vincent de Paul is an international voluntary organization in the Catholic Church, founded in 1833 for the sanctification of its members by personal service to the poor. The first U.S. society was founded in 1845 in Saint Louis, Missouri. "The Beginnings of the Society of St. Vincent de Paul," https://ssvpusa.org/about-us/history/, accessed March 1, 2021.

68. The Carmen Velásquez Memorial Award was given to an individual who had done extraordinary work with the local migrant community. The award was developed after Carmen's death in 1985 and distributed until the 1990s by the Indiana Task Force for Migratory Affairs. "Velasquez Award Presented to Francie Metzger," *Call–Leader* (Elwood, IN), July 2, 1998.

69. Republican Robert D. Orr (1917–2004) served as Indiana's governor from 1981 to 1989. "List of Governors," Indiana Historical Bureau, https://www.in.gov/history/, accessed June 29, 2021.

70. Holy Week in Christianity is the week before Easter. "Holy Week," *Encyclopedia Britannica*.

71. In April 1971 staff from AMOS (Associated Migrant Opportunity Services) and supporters of migrant farmworkers' rights organized a march from Marion, Indiana, to the governor's mansion in Indianapolis, which is roughly sixty-one miles. "Migrants Hope to Meet with Gov. Whitcomb," *Kokomo Tribune* (Kokomo, IN), April 5, 1971.

Chapter 3

Gaining Visibility and Power, 1970–1989

1. Robert Aponte and Brenda Graves, "Latinos in Indiana: On the Throes of Growth," Statistical Brief No. 11, July 1999, Julian Samora Research Institute, Michigan State University–East Lansing, https://jsri.msu.edu/upload/statistical-briefs/cifras11.pdf., accessed March 1, 2021.

2. Emiliano Aguilar, "The East Chicago Washington High School Walkout, 50 Years Later," Indiana Historical Society blog, October 28, 2020, https://indianahistory.org/blog/the-east-chicago-washington-high-school-walkout-50-years-later/; Samuel Wyatt, "Latins Plan for '74," *Latin Times* (East Chicago, IN), December 23, 1973; Charles Sterling, *Times* (Munster, IN), October 7, 1970, Newspapers.com, Ancestry.

3. Associated Press, "Stranded Migrants Demand Assistance," *South Bend Tribune* (South Bend, IN), October 8, 1974.

4. "1973 Kokomo–Howard County Health Department Annual Report," *Kokomo Tribune* (Kokomo, IN), July 21, 1974.

5. "Johnson County Churches Form 'Migrant Ministry,'" *Daily Journal* (Franklin, IN), April 30, 1969.

6. Carl Allsup, "Concerned Latin Organizations," in *Forging a Community: The Latino Experience in Northwest Indiana, 1919–1975*, eds. Edward J. Escobar and James B. Lane, vol. 2 (Chicago, IL: Cattails Press, 1987), 252–55.

7. Maria Luisa Tishner Oral History Interview, 2016, Indiana Latino History Project, SC 3479, Indiana Historical Society.

8. It is likely that Raúl was part of the Bracero Program (1942–64). See Chapter 2 in this book, "1940–1949: War Relief, Military Service, and the Arrival of Puerto Ricans."

9. The Texas agricultural sector produces cotton, hay, vegetables, citrus, corn, wheat, peanuts, pecans, sorghum, and rice. Its livestock industry is comprised of cattle, sheep, goats, and horses. Mission, Texas, is a large citrus-producing area, most notable for ruby red grapefruit. "Texas Agriculture Facts," Texas Department of Agriculture, https://www.texasagriculture.gov/Portals/0/DigArticle/1930/Ag%20Week%20Fact%20Sheet%203%2013%2013.pdf, accessed April 30, 2021.

10. Brooks Foods started as Summit Products in 1925. The company's name was changed to Brooks Foods in 1956. It closed in 1997. "Brooks Foods Will Shut Down in Mount Summit," *Star Press* (Muncie, IN), April 24, 1997.

11. Seasonal agricultural workers lived in temporary onsite housing areas called camps. Camps were provided by the farmer or company that owned the farmland. Onsite housing often consisted of a one-bedroom house with minimal utilities. "Housing in Rural America: A Historical Look Back," National Agriculture Library, https://www.nal.usda.gov/exhibits/ipd/ruralusa/exhibits/show/housing/farmworker, accessed April 30, 2021.

12. The Corpus Christi Produce Company was established in 1946. Corpus Christi Produce, https://ccproducehd.com/, accessed April 30, 2021.

13. Corpus Christi is called the "Sparkling City by the Sea." W. F. Strong and Emily Donahue, "How Many of these Texas City Nicknames Do You Know?" in *Texas Standard: The National Daily News Show of Texas*, July 29, 2015, https://www.texasstandard.org/stories/how-many-of-these-texas-city-nicknames-do-you-know/, accessed July 23, 2021.

14. Robert Salinas's maternal grandmother was Irene Velásquez Clark (1921–2009), who married his step-grandfather, Julian G. Clark Jr. (1926–2011) in 1945. His biological maternal grandfather was Tony Amaro (1920–2011).

15. The first class for Kokomo High School, located on the corner of Armstrong and Taylor, was admitted in 1872. In 1898 the original building burned down, and a second building was erected on the corner of Market and Sycamore. In 1914 the second school building suffered the same fate, after which a new building was dedicated in 1917, located at 303 East Superior Street. Today this third building houses Central Middle School. The current campus of Kokomo High School was built in 1968. In 1984 it was merged with Haworth High School. In 2021 it is the only high school in the Kokomo–Center Township School Corporation. "History of KHS," Kokomo School Corporation, https://khs.kokomoschools.com/about_us/history_of_khs, accessed April 30, 2021.

16. Incorporated as a city in 1891, Elwood lies in Madison and Tipton Counties, Indiana, south of Marion and north of Indianapolis. Suspected at one time to be Indiana's Ku Klux Klan headquarters, Elwood was long referred to as a "sundown town," meaning that people of color would be in danger if they were seen there after sunset. In the 1970s the Klan's grand dragon, William Scott, resided in Elwood. Rebecca R. Bibbs, "Madison County Communities Strive to Overcome 'Sundown Town' Reputation," *Herald Bulletin* (Anderson, IN), April 3, 2016, online at https://www.heraldbulletin.com/.

17. *Pepinos* is Spanish for cucumbers.

18. Roosevelt School, located on West Barkdol Street by Northside Park in Kokomo, Indiana, was an elementary school that closed in the mid- to late-1990s due to decreased enrollment. "Kokomo School Corporation History," Kokomo School Corporation, https://www.kokomoschools.com/our_district/history, accessed April 30, 2021.

19. Kokomo Transmission is a Chrysler automobile factory that was established in 1956. It is located at 2401 South Reed Road in Kokomo. "Kokomo Transmission Plant," Stellantis, https://media.stellantisnorthamerica.com/newsrelease.do?id=322&mid=, accessed April 30, 2021.

20. A subsidiary of General Motors, Delco Electronics Corporation was an automotive electronics design and manufacturing company. Delco is an acronym for Dayton Engineering Laboratories Company, which innovated automotive electric systems. "Delphi's History in Kokomo," *Kokomo Tribune* (Kokomo, IN), October 10, 2006, https://www.kokomotribune.com/news/local_news/delphi-s-history-in-kokomo/article_8462da5a-4c59-5dbb-9ef5-abde055f720f.html, accessed April 30, 2021.

21. The Howard County Corrections Division is located at 1800 West Markland Avenue, Kokomo.

22. A landline phone is a traditional phone line that uses a metal or optical wire telephone line, connected to a jack in the wall for transmission. In comparison, mobile or cellular phones use radio waves for transmission. See *Merriam–Webster* online.

23. Rodger Lee "Peanut" Fain (1944–2003), Death Certificate, filed January 27, 2003, State of Indiana, Department of Health, State No. 100635, Ancestry.

24. The Bilingual Services Department of the South Bend Community School Corporation provides the following programs for families within the South Bend school system: English as a new language, tutorial and support services, and a bilingual/migrant summer program. "Bilingual Services," South Bend Community School

Corporation, http://sb.school/district_information/departments/bilingual_services, accessed April 30, 2021.

25. Evan Bayh served as Indiana's governor from 1989 to 1997. The Twenty-First Century Scholars program was created during his administration. The Twenty-First Century Scholars program offers students up to four years of undergraduate tuition at a participating Indiana public college or university, provided that the student maintains a 2.5 GPA or higher, completes a Scholar Success Program, graduates with a high school diploma (at least a Core 40 diploma), pledges not to use illegal drugs or alcohol, or to commit a crime or delinquent act. See "Indiana Governor Evan Bayh (b. 1955)," Indiana Historical Bureau, https://www.in.gov/history/about-indiana-history-and-trivia/governors-portraits/list-of-governors/indiana-governor-evan-bayh-b-1955/, accessed March 1, 2021.

26. Jackson Middle School is a "Project Lead the Way" magnet school in the South Bend Community School Corporation for students in grades five through eight. It is located at 5001 South Miami Road in South Bend, Indiana. "Jackson Middle School," South Bend Community School Corporation, http://jackson.sb.school/, accessed April 30, 2021.

Chapter 4
A New Era of Growth, Diversity, and Advocacy, 1980–2020

1. Immigration Reform and Control Act of 1986, S.1200, 99th Cong. (1986).

2. Caroline Mimbs Nyce and Chris Bodenner, "Looking Back at Amnesty under Reagan," Atlantic, May 23, 2016, https://www.theatlantic.com/notes/2016/05/thirty-years-after-the-immigration-reform-and-control-act/482364/.

3. Michael Satchell, "New Law Helps Some, Hurts Others," Indianapolis Star (Indianapolis, IN), January 11, 1987.

4. Rachel Thelin and Dona Sapp, "Indiana Latino Community Outreach Initiative: Indiana Latino Community Profile and Survey of Latino-Serving Organizations," Indiana Latino Institute, http://indianalatinoinstitute.org/wp-content/uploads/2016/07/ILI_Latino-Community-Profile-and-Organization-Survey_FINAL_v1.pdf, accessed August 3, 2021; Rachel Strange, "Exploring Hoosier Minority Groups: Indiana's Hispanic Population," IN Context 14, no. 4 (2013), http://www.incontext.indiana.edu/2013/july-aug/article3.asp; Robert Aponte and Brenda Graves, "Latinos in Indiana: On the Throes of Growth," Statistical Brief No. 11, July 1999, Julian Samora Research Institute, Michigan State University–East Lansing, https://jsri.msu.edu/upload/statistical-briefs/cifras11.pdf, accessed March 1, 2021.

5. Statistics are from Stats Indiana, the statistical data utility for the State of Indiana, developed and maintained since 1985 by the Indiana Business Research Center at Indiana University's Kelley School of Business. Support is or has been provided by the State of Indiana, Lilly Endowment, the Indiana Department of Workforce Development, and Indiana University, https://www.stats.indiana.edu/profiles/profiles.asp?scope_choice=a&county_changer=18000, accessed May 19, 2021.

6. Gabriel "Gabe" Eloy Aguirre (1935–2017). "In Memoriam: Sani-Serv's Gabriel Aguirre," Food Service Equipment Reports, December 13, 2017, https://www.fermag.com/articles/8086-in-memoriam-saniservs-gabriel-aguirre/, accessed March 18, 2021.

7. Jeff Swiatek, "Trip Is a Chance to Learn about HIV Virus," Indianapolis Star (Indianapolis, IN), August 23, 1992.

8. "Panel Focuses on AIDS and Women," Indianapolis Star, November 7, 1990.

9. Anonymous testing occurs when personal information is collected and/or recorded for a medical test, as for HIV/AIDS. A number or code is assigned to the individual being tested so that no one can access the identity of the person being tested. "About HIV," Center for Disease Control and Prevention, https://www.cdc.gov/hiv/basics/whatishiv.html, accessed April 30, 2021.

10. Rann Destefano, "Chris Gonzalez: LGBTQ Activist," Encyclopedia of Indianapolis, https://indyencyclopedia.org/, accessed February 23, 2022.

11. Stats Indiana, https://www.stats.indiana.edu/index.asp, accessed August 2, 2021.

12. Thelin and Sapp, "Indiana Latino Community Outreach Initiative."

13. "Mario Rodríguez," Indianapolis International Airport, https://www.ind.com/about/leadership/senior-leadership/mario-rodriguez, accessed March 4, 2021.

14. Thelin and Sapp, "Indiana Latino Community Outreach Initiative."

15. Suzette Hackney, "Hackney: Kids on Winning Robotics Team Told 'Go Back to Mexico,'" IndyStar (Indianapolis, IN), March 17, 2017, indystar.com.

16. Michael Puente, "Latino Group Joins Lawsuits Against Indiana over Immigration Law," last modified December 22, 2011, WBEZChicago, https://www.wbez.org/stories/latino-group-joins-lawsuits-against-indiana-over-immigration-law/19c03c52-adb5-4eb5-9a96-4915f33b54a8, accessed March 4, 2021.

17. "Our History," Indiana Latino Institute, http://indianalatinoinstitute.org/about-us/our-history/, accessed March 4, 2021.

18. Thelin and Sapp, "Indiana Latino Community Outreach Initiative."

19. Saint Christopher Catholic Church, established in 1937, is located at 5301 West 16th Street, Indianapolis, Indiana. St. Christopher Parish, https://sites.google.com/stchrisindy.org/st-christopher-parish/home, accessed April 30, 2021.

20. Father D. Michael Welch retired as pastor of Saint Christopher parish in Indianapolis in 2014. John Shaughnesy, "The Memories Flow from Father Welch's 50 Years as a Priest, Criterion Edition Online (September 4, 2020), https://www.archindy.org/criterion/local/2020/09-04/welch.html.

21. On July 28, 1821, Lima, Peru, proclaimed independence from the Spanish Empire. Peruvians celebrate their independence on two consecutive days. The first is a national celebration and the second is a day of family outings. "Peru," Encyclopedia Britannica, https://www.britannica.com/.

22. Wishard Memorial Hospital in Indianapolis, Indiana, originally City Hospital, was established in 1859 to treat smallpox, but was later used as a military hospital to treat wounded soldiers during the Civil War. Following the war, it became a city-owned charity hospital. It was renamed Wishard Memorial Hospital in 1975 to honor Doctor William N. Wishard, the hospital's director in the 1880s. The hospital continues in part due to a $40 million donation by Sidney and Lois Eskenazi to rebuild the facility. When the new building opened in 2013, the hospital was renamed in their honor. "History," Eskenazi Health, https://www.eskenazihealth.edu, accessed August 2, 2021.

23. AIDS is the acronym for Acquired Immunodeficiency Syndrome. HIV can lead to AIDS if not treated. "40 Years of Progress: It's Time to End the HIV Epidemic, Center for Disease Control and Prevention, https://www.cdc.gov/hiv/default.html, accessed August 9, 2021.

24. Indiana Latino Institute, Inc. is an Internal Revenue Code Section 501(c)(3) nonprofit agency established in 2001. It is the only statewide organization committed to serving Indiana Latino communities. "Our History," Indiana Latino Institute, http://indianalatinoinstitute.org/about-us/our-history/, accessed April 30, 2021.

25. The Master Settlement Agreement is the largest civil litigation settlement in U.S. history. It began on November 23, 1998, and involved major cigarette manufacturers in forty-six states and six U.S. jurisdictions. The manufacturers agreed to make annual payments to the states, compensating them for taxpayer money spent on healthcare costs connected to tobacco-related illness. "The Master Settlement Agreement," National Association of Attorneys General, https://www.naag.org/our-work/naag-center-for-tobacco-and-public-health/the-master-settlement-agreement/, accessed April 30, 2021; "Master Settlement Agreement," Truth Initiative, https://truthinitiative.org/who-we-are/our-history/master-settlement-agreement, accessed April 30, 2021.

26. This statement refers to Indiana State Public Laws 141-2012, 70-2014, 53-2014, and 231-2015, which have been codified as Indiana Code 7.1-5-12. "Indiana's Statewide Smoke-Free Air Law: FAQs," Breathe Easy Indiana, https://www.breatheindiana.com/faq, accessed April 30, 2021; "Chapter 12: Prohibition on Smoking," Justia.com, https://statecodesfiles.justia.com/indiana/2016/title-7.1/article-5/chapter-12/chapter-12.pdf, accessed April 30, 2021.

27. The Indiana Senate Page Program, an interactive educational experience, is designed for students in grades six through twelve to learn about state government. Under state law, Hoosier students may receive an excused absence from school to serve as a Senate Page one day per legislative session. "Page Program," Indiana State Republicans, https://www.indianasenaterepublicans.com/page-program, accessed April 30, 2021.

28. Circle Centre Mall, owned by Simon Property Group, is located in downtown Indianapolis. It features more than one hundred retailers, a movie theater, restaurants, nightclubs, and connecting hotels. "About Circle Centre Mall," Circle Centre Mall, https://www.simon.com/mall/circle-centre-mall/about, accessed April 30, 2021.

29. House Legislative Latino Page Day was later renamed Indiana Latino Legislative Summit by Indiana House Representative Christina Hale. "State Rep. Candelaria Reardon Hosts 13th Annual Latino Fellowship Day at the Statehouse," Indiana House Democratic Caucus, https://indianahousedemocrats.org/news-media/state-rep.-mara-candelaria-reardon-hosts-13th-annual-latino-fellowship-day-at-the-statehouse, accessed May 18, 2021.

30. Goshen is a city in Elkhart County on the northern border of Indiana, with a population of 31,719 as of the 2010 census; 19.33 percent of its population self-reported as Latino. Bremen is a city in Marshall County in north central Indiana, with a population of 4,588 as of the 2010 census; 18 percent of its population self-reported as Latino. Plymouth is also a city in Marshall County, with a population of 10,033 as of the 2010 census; 20 percent of its population self-reported as Latino. "Quick Facts: Elkhart County, Indiana; Elkhart, Indiana," United States Census Bureau, https://www.census.gov/quickfacts/fact/table/elkhartcountyindiana,elkhartcityindiana/PST045219, accessed April 30, 2021; Town of Bremen, https://www.townofbremen.com/, accessed April 30, 2021; "Quick Facts: Marshall County, Indiana, Elkhart County, Indiana, Elkhart, Indiana," United States Census Bureau, https://www.census.gov/quickfacts/fact/table/marshallcountyindiana,elkhartcountyindiana,elkhartcityindiana/PST045219, accessed April 30, 2021; Plymouth, Indiana, https://www.plymouthin.com/, accessed April 30, 2021.

31. The bicentennial celebration for Indiana's statehood (1816–2016) included a torch relay through all ninety-two counties in the state, covering 3,200 miles over a five-week period. Torchbearers were chosen by their counties from submitted nominations. "Torch Relay," IN.gov, https://www.in.gov/ibc/torchrelay/index.htm, accessed April 30, 2021.

32. The Sagamore of the Wabash award was created during the term of Governor Ralph Gates (1945–49). It is the highest honor bestowed by the Indiana governor and is a personal tribute given to those who have rendered a distinguished service to the state or the governor. "Sagamore of the Wabash," IN.gov, https://www.in.gov/portal/files/Sagamore.pdf, accessed April 30, 2021.

33. The intersection of Lafayette Boulevard and West Western Avenue in South Bend is a few blocks from the Studebaker National Museum at 201 Chapin Street. Studebaker National Museum, https://www.studebakermuseum.org/, accessed April 30, 2021.

34. Bendix Woods County Park is located on Timothy Road, south of U.S. 20, in New Carlisle, Indiana. "Bendix Woods Nature Preserve," IN.gov, https://www.in.gov/dnr/nature-preserves/files/np-Bendix.pdf, accessed April 30, 2021.

35. César E. Chávez (1927–1993), was a prominent union leader and labor organizer who protested via non-violent means, such as boycotts, marches, and hunger strikes. He founded the National Farm Workers Association in 1962. "The Story of César Chávez," United Farm Workers, https://ufw.org/research/history/story-cesar-chavez/, accessed April 2021. Greg Chávez is no relation to César Chávez.

36. Potawatomi Park, a city park that includes a pool, zoo, and conservatory, is located at 321 East Walter Street, South Bend. "Potawatomi Park," City of South Bend, https://sbvpa.org/places/potawatomi-park/, accessed April 30, 2021.

37. The "economic situation" referenced was caused by Operation Bootstrap, a series of federal projects that shifted the economy of Puerto Rico from agriculture to manufacturing. Prior to this, the Puerto Rican economy was largely supported by sugar cane plantations. This economic shift caused 43,000 Puerto Ricans to emigrate between 1950 and 1959. Matt Rosenberg, "Geography of Puerto Rico," Thought Co., https://www.thoughtco.com/geography-of-puerto-rico-1435563, accessed April 30, 2021.

38. The American Civil Rights Movement was a national protest movement against racial segregation and discrimination during the 1950s and 1960s. The Women's Rights Movement of the 1960s was the second wave of activism in the United States addressing discrimination against women. The first wave took place in 1848. "The African American Civil Rights Movement," Library of Congress, https://loc.gov/item/ihas.200197396, accessed May 5, 2021; "History of the Women's Rights Movement," National Women's History Alliance, https://nationalwomenshistoryalliance.org/history-of-the-womens-rights-movement/, accessed May 4, 2021.

39. The Young Lords was a Puerto Rican nationalist group active in several U.S. cities, notably Chicago and New York City. It was organized in the 1960s by José "Cha Cha" Jiménez as a civil and human rights movement. "Young Lords in Lincoln Park," Grand Valley State University, https://www.gvsu.edu/library/specialcollections/young-lords-in-lincoln-park-22.htm, accessed April 30, 2021.

40. The Chicano Movement of the 1960s was a civil rights movement that extended from the Mexican American Civil Rights Movement, which had formed following World War II. Both of these movements addressed negative ethnic stereotypes of Latinos in the American consciousness, as well as discrimination in public and private institutions. "The Chicano Civil Rights Movement," Library of Congress, https://www.loc.gov/item/ihas.200197398/, accessed April 30, 2021.

41. Wesleyan University, a liberal arts university in Middletown, Connecticut, was founded in 1831. Originally open to both men and women, it became an all-male university in 1912. The university began to actively recruit students of color in the 1960s and became coeducational again in 1970, once again accepting women students. "History of Wesleyan," Wesleyan University, https://www.wesleyan.edu/about/history-traditions/index.html, accessed April 30, 2021.

42. The American Indian Movement, an advocacy group, was founded in 1968 to address sovereignty, treaty issues, spirituality, and leadership, along with incidents of police harassment and racism. Dartmouth College, a private, Ivy League university in Hanover, New Hampshire, was founded in 1769 as a school to educate Native Americans in Christian theology and the English way of life. Originally a men's institution, Dartmouth became coeducational in 1972. "The American Indian Movement, 1968–1978," Digital Public Library of America, https://dp.la/primary-source-sets/the-american-indian-movement-1968-1978, accessed April 30, 2021; "History and Traditions," Dartmouth College, https://home.dartmouth.edu/life-community/explore-green/history-traditions, accessed April 30, 2021.

43. The Hispanic Education Center was established in 1987 and was merged into *La Plaza* in 2004. "Hispanic Education Center," Buzzfile, 2021, https://www.buzzfile.com/business/Hispanic-Education-Center-317-890-3292, accessed August 3, 2021; "History," La Plaza: Strengthening Youth, Families, and Community, https://www.laplazaindy.org/history/, accessed August 3, 2021.

44. *Fiesta* Indianapolis began in 1981 as a celebration of Latino culture in Indiana with an annual event in September of music, dancing, food, children's activities, a health and wellness fair, and community service booths. Dan Briere, Charles Guthrie, and Mary Moore, "Hispanics," in *Encyclopedia of Indianapolis*, David J. Bodenhamer and Robert G. Barrows, eds. (Bloomington: Indiana University Press, 1994), 684.

45. *La Plaza* was formed from the merger of the Hispanic Education Center, Fiesta Indianapolis, and *El Centro Hispano* in 2004. Among other functions, it serves as the liaison between Latinos and the larger Indianapolis community. "History," La Plaza: Strengthening Youth, Families, and Community.

46. This statement refers to Internal Revenue Code Section 501(c)(6). "Business Leagues," IRS, https://www.irs.gov/charities-non-profits/other-non-profits/business-leagues, accessed August 3, 2021.

47. After a long career in business and higher education, Sue Ellspermann served as Indiana's fiftieth lieutenant governor from 2013 to 2016. As of 2021 she was president of Ivy Tech Community College of Indiana. "Dr. Sue Ellspermann," Ivy Tech Community College, https://www.ivytech.edu/president/, accessed May 4, 2021.

48. Bishop Gerald A. Gettelfinger was a priest and bishop in the Archdiocese of Indianapolis from 1961–89. He was then appointed bishop of the Diocese of Evansville until his retirement in 2010. U.S Highway 231 is a north-south highway running from Indiana to Florida. Sean Gallagher, "Bishop Gettelfinger Reflects on 50 Years of Ministry," *Criterion Online Edition* (July 1, 2011), https://www.archindy.org/criterion/local/2011/07-01/gettelfinger.html; "U.S. 231—Indiana to Florida: How a Highway Grew," Highway History, U.S. Department of Transportation, Federal Highway Administration, https://www.fhwa.dot.gov/infrastructure/us231.cfm, accessed August 3, 2021; "Quick Facts: Jasper City, Indiana; Dubois County, Indiana," United States Census Bureau, https://www.census.gov/quickfacts/fact/table/jaspercityindiana,duboiscountyindiana/HCN010212, accessed August 3, 2021; "Quick Facts: Huntingburg City, Indiana," United States Census Bureau, https://www.census.gov/quickfacts/huntingburgcityindiana, accessed August 3, 2021.

49. The Guadalupe Center was originally founded in September 1999 in Jasper, Indiana. Its purpose was to provide aid to Latino immigrants in establishing themselves in the United States. In 2000 its headquarters moved to Huntingburg, Indiana, where it remains under the support of the Archdiocese of Evansville. *The Guadalupe Center* 11, no. 3 (May–June 2013), http://www.evdio.org/uploads/2/6/3/0/26308718/newsletter_may-june_2013.pdf.

50. Maura G. Robinson is a sociologist who founded Inclusion and Beyond, a service that aids businesses in forming a diverse workforce. Russell G. Lloyd Jr. served as mayor of Evansville, Indiana, from 2000–3. Inclusion and Beyond, Inc.: A Full Service Diversity, Equity, and Inclusion Company, https://www.inclusionandbeyond.com/, accessed August 3, 2021; "Evansville's Mayors," City of Evansville, Indiana, https://www.evansvillegov.org/city/topic/index.php?topicid=1&structureid=123, accessed August 3, 2021.

51. HOLA (Hospitality and Outreach for Latin Americans) is an organization established in 2002 in Evansville, Indiana. Its purpose is to celebrate and include in the community incoming Latinos in the southern Indiana area. HOLA, https://holaevansville.org/, accessed August 3, 2021.

52. The Southwest Indiana Chamber was established in 1915. More than one hundred years later in 2016, the Latino Chamber Alliance formally became part of this group, reflecting the changing demographics of the state and the growth of the Latino community. "Our History and Milestones," Latino Chamber Alliance, https://swinchamber.com/latino-chamber-alliance/, accessed August 3, 2021.

Conclusion
Capturing Hoosier Latino History: A Beginning

1. Juan Gonzalez, *Harvest of Empire: A History of Latinos in America* (New York: Penguin Books, 2001; rev. ed., 2011), 96.

2. Sujey Vega, *Latino Heartland: Of Borders and Belonging in the Midwest* (New York: New York University Press, 2015), 26–27.

Panels from *Be Heard: Latino Experiences in Indiana* exhibition, 2018, Indiana Historical Society, Indianapolis

Acknowledgments

The Indiana Historical Society is indebted to Lilly Endowment for making possible its Indiana Latino History Project. The fruits of this project now include a growing collection of oral history interviews and transcriptions, genealogical and historical data, and photos, called the Indiana Latino History Collection, which are available in the IHS Digital Collection. They also encompass the highly successful 2018 exhibition *Be Heard: Latino Experiences in Indiana* and a traveling exhibit based on it, as well as several blog pieces on the IHS website, and this book, *Hoosier Latinos: A Century of Struggle, Service, and Success*.

Hoosier Latinos was built upon a foundation of collaboration among many individual participants and community supporters of the Indiana Latino History Project that began in the summer of 2016. The Indiana Historical Society is grateful for everyone who has helped promote this project and helped to develop the historical narrative it is engendering. Oral history contributors to the project stretched from the northwestern part of the state to the southern parts of Indiana. These participants represent the wide spectrum of Indiana's Latinx community. Special thanks go to the members of the Old Timers of Indiana Harbor, a Latino social group. Some of these members are children of early residents of Indiana Harbor, whose presence there dates back as early as 1918. Among them is the family of project curator and author Nicole Martinez–LeGrand. The Old Timers have been integral in helping her find and develop trusting relationships with prospective families for this initiative. The Indiana Latino History Collection in the IHS's William Henry Smith Memorial Library would not have been possible without their sharing and donations of early photos and oral recollections.

The project's participants and supporters from 2016 through 2020 include the following individuals and families: Miriam Acevedo–Davis, Amanda Aguilera, Judith Aguilera, Tom Álvarez, Peter Ayala, Antonio "Tony" Barreda, the children of Raúl Bolaños (Angela Byrne and Michael Bolaños), Lydia Castillo, Marilu Castillo, Gregorio "Greg" Chávez, Michael Del Castillo, Carmen DeRusha, the children of Feliciano and María Espinoza (Sylvia Clark, Rick Espinoza, Connie Hamm, and others), the children of Francisco and Consuelo Figueroa (including Lupe Figueroa, Irene Osorio, and others), Edward Garza, Richard Garza, Adrienne Gómez, Rosemarie Gómez, Enrique González and Harlon Wilson, Tamara Lee, Hope Logston, Frederick "Fred" Ruiz Maravilla, Edward Medina, Dwan Moreno, Rick and Liliana Morfin, Miguel Olguin (and daughter), Tomacita Pérez, Horace Piñon, Raúl and Rogelia Piñon, Maura Robinson, Robert Salinas, Maryori Duarte Sheffield, María Luisa Tishner, Sandra Valdés, the children and grandchild of María Carmen and Albert Velásquez (including Zach Adamson, Mary Margaret Velásquez de Bertram, Celestina "Tina" Velásquez Masterson, Catherine "Cathy" Velásquez Mitchell, Charles Velásquez, and others), and Alfonso and Daniela Vidal.

Past and present staff members of the Indiana Historical Society were also integral in providing encouragement and expertise for building the foundations of the Indiana Latino History Collection, the exhibits, and this book. Deep gratitude from the authors of this book and the exhibitions, Nicole Martinez–LeGrand and Daniel Gonzales, goes out to: President and CEO Jody Blankenship and former President and CEO John Herbst; Vice Presidents Suzanne Hahn, Jeff Matsuoka, Amy Lamb, and Andrew Halter; Library and Archives staff: Lindsay Borman, Paul Brockman, Ramona Duncan–Huse, Stephanie Gowler, Maire Gurevitz, Nadia Kousari, Kathy Lechuga, Jasmine Long, Eric Mundell, Jordan Ryan, Michael Stauffer, Susan Sutton, and David Turk; Development and Membership team members: Wendy Adams and her on-call transcription experts, Nancy Germano and Susan Darnell, as well as Tom Borman, Emily Rawlinson, and Sarah Sankovitch; Jeff Mills and his Exhibitions team members: Tabitha Cravens and Angela Wolfgram; Bethany Hrachovec and her team in Education and Community Engagement: Beth Brandon, Jonnie Fox, Callie McCune, and Lauren Peightel; Tamara Hemmerlein of Local History Services and Marianne Sheline of External Engagement; Marketing staff: Kim Easton, Rachel Hill Ponko, and Chelsea Sutton; IHS Press staff: Teresa Baer and Natalie Burriss, who helped to plan, compile, organize, and edit this book; Kathy Breen who created the index for the book; and Ray Boomhower.

The authors and editors are very grateful for the opening essay contributed by Professor Sujey Vega of Arizona State University. Many thanks also go to IHS designers Stacy Simmer, Chris McCoy, and Isabelle Kroeker for the thoughtful design of this book. Finally, thanks go to Alan Rowe, Supervisor–Archivist, Indiana University Health, Indianapolis, for his research assistance; and to Luke Steele and Jordan Ryan for their German translation advice.

Ballet Folklorico Dancers from East Chicago, Indiana, ca. 1960s. Lupe Figueroa is the second woman from the right.

Glossary

Chicano

An American male of Mexican descent. Its first known use was in 1947. Chicana refers to females, and sometimes Chicanx has been used to refer to Mexican Americans of all genders. The term was popularized in the mid-1960s as the Chicano political movement emerged to push for civil rights and recognition for long-standing communities of Mexican descent. While this term is largely associated with Mexican Americans, some Latinos of other nationalities have embraced it believing they share a common political and social struggle.

Hispanic

A descriptor for someone of Spanish descent or from a Spanish-speaking Latin American country. The use of this term was popularized when the Richard Nixon presidential administration used the term in official government offices and positions created to serve this growing community. The term "Hispanic" excludes those from Latin American countries who do not speak Spanish, such as Brazilians.

Hoosierlandia

An informal word in Spanish for Indiana or "Land of Hoosiers."

Latino

A collective description for people of Spanish-speaking countries of Latin America who were once colonized as part of the Spanish Empire. This term was commonly used at the end of the twentieth century in response to the term Hispanic, as it includes non-Spanish speaking Latin Americans from countries such as Brazil, where Portuguese is spoken.

Latinx

A gender neutral and inclusive term for Latino (male version) or Latina (female version). This became more prominent in the late 2010s.

Mexican American

A person born in the United States with one or both parents of Mexican ancestry. May also indicate a person born in Mexico who has become an American citizen.

Sources

Merriam–Webster online. | Rodriguez, Roberto. "The Origins and History of the Chicano Movement," JSRI Occasional Paper #7. East Lansing: Michigan State University, Julian Samora Research Institute, 1966. | Stavans, Ilan. *Latinos in the United States: What Everyone Needs to Know*. New York: Oxford University Press, 2018. | Vega, Sujey. *Latino Heartland: Of Borders and Belonging in the Midwest*. New York: New York University Press, 2015.

Rudy Gómez of East Chicago in uniform during World War II, 1944

Selected Bibliography

Books

Baer, M. Teresa. *Indianapolis: A City of Immigrants*. Indianapolis: Indiana Historical Society Press, 2012.

Bodenhamer, David J., and Robert G. Barrows, eds. *Encyclopedia of Indianapolis*. Bloomington: Indiana University Press, 1994.

Escobar, Edward J., and James B. Lane, eds. Calumet Regional Studies Series. Vol. 2, *Forging a Community: The Latino Experience in Northwest Indiana, 1919–1975*. Chicago: Cattails Press, 1987.

Gonzalez, Juan. *Harvest of Empire: A History of Latinos in America*. New York: Penguin Books, 2011.

Taylor, Paul S. The American Immigration Collection. Vol. 7, *Mexican Labor in the United States: Chicago and the Calumet Region*. New York: Arno Press, 1970.

Taylor, Robert M., and Connie A. McBirney. *Peopling Indiana: The Ethnic Experience*. Indianapolis: Indiana Historical Society, 1996.

Vargas, Zaragosa. *Proletarians of the North: A History of Mexican Industrial Workers in Detroit and the Midwest, 1917–1933*. Oakland: University of California Press, 1999.

Vega, Sujey. *Latino Heartland: Of Borders and Belonging in the Midwest*. New York: New York University Press, 2015.

Documents and Collections

Aponte, Robert, and Brenda Graves. "Latinos in Indiana: On the Throes of Growth." Statistical Brief No. 11, July 1999. Julian Samora Research Institute, Michigan State University–East Lansing.

Guthrie, Charles C. "Hispanic Indianapolis: Personal Histories from an Emerging Community." Oral History Project, 1990, BV 3523. Indiana Historical Society.

Martinez–LeGrand, Nicole. Indiana Latino History Project. William Henry Smith Memorial Library, Indiana Historical Society.

Thelin, Rachel, and Dona Sapp. "Indiana Latino Community Outreach Initiative: Indiana Latino Community Profile and Survey of Latino-Serving Organizations." Indiana Latino Institute, 2016.

Wilson, Elizabeth N. "Notes on the Early History of the International Institute of Gary." International Institute Papers. Calumet Regional Archives, Indiana University–Northwest, September 1932.

Articles

Fraire, John. "Mexicans Playing Baseball in Indiana Harbor, 1925–1942." *Indiana Magazine of History* 110, no. 2 (2014).

Library of Congress. "Becoming Part of the United States." In Immigration and Relocation in U.S. History, Mexican.

———. "The Chicano Civil Rights Movement."

Nyce, Caroline Mimbs, and Chris Bodenner. "Looking Back at Amnesty under Reagan." *Atlantic*, May 23, 2016.

Oropeza, Lorena. "Latinos in World War II: Fighting on Two Fronts." National Park Service.

Strange, Rachel. "Exploring Hoosier Minority Groups: Indiana's Hispanic Population." *IN Context* 14, no. 4 (2013).

Legislation

Immigration Reform and Control Act of 1986, S.1200, 99th Cong. (1968).

Title VII—Bilingual Education Programs, Pub. L. No. 90-247, 81 Stat. 816 (1968).

Fiestas Patrias queens of past and present in East Chicago, 2001. The woman in the wheelchair is the first queen, María del Refugio Ramírez.

Appendix

A Primer On Latin America

Latin America

A collective group of countries and dependencies in the Western Hemisphere that were colonized by Spain and once were a part of the Spanish Empire; includes the countries of Mexico, Central America, South America, and the Caribbean.

Countries of Latin America by Region

Central America

Southernmost region of North America, includes: Belize, Costa Rica, El Salvador, Guatemala, Honduras, Nicaragua, and Panama

South America

Includes Argentina, Bolivia, Brazil, Chile, Colombia, Ecuador, French Guiana, Guyana, Paraguay, Peru, Suriname, Uruguay, and Venezuela

The Caribbean

Antigua and Barbuda, Bahamas, Barbados, Cuba, Dominica, Dominican Republic, Grenada, Haiti, Jamaica, Saint Kitts and Nevis, Saint Lucia, Saint Vincent and the Grenadines, Trinidad and Tobago

Territories

Territories that are considered part of the Caribbean are dependencies of other countries. These include: Puerto Rico (USA); Virgin Islands (USA and UK); Anguilla, Cayman Islands, Monserrat, and Turks and Caicos Islands (UK); Guadeloupe, Martinique, Saint Barthelemy (aka Saint Bart's), and Saint Martin (France); and Aruba, Caribbean Netherlands, Curacao, and Sint Maarten (Netherlands).

Languages Spoken in Latin America

African languages, Dutch, English, French, Indigenous languages, Portuguese, Spanish, and Creole (a combination of Indigenous, African, and European languages)

Population and Indigenous Languages of Latin America and the Caribbean

In 2021, according to statistics from the United Nations, more than 660 million individuals lived in Latin America and the Caribbean altogether. Of these, some 40 million speak Indigenous languages, of which there are hundreds. In the fifteenth and sixteenth centuries Europeans documented the following Indigenous languages and where they were spoken (by country designations of today): Aymara (Bolivia, northern Chile, and southern Peru), Guaraní (Argentina, Brazil, Bolivia, and Paraguay), Maya (Belize, Guatemala, Honduras, and southern Mexico), Náhuatl (El Salvador and Mexico), Taíno (Cuba, Dominican Republic, Haiti, and Puerto Rico), and Quechua (northern Argentina, Bolivia, southern Colombia, Ecuador, and Peru).

Sources

Encyclopedia Britannica. | "A Treasury of Tongues." *Unesco Courier* special issue (July 1983), https://unesdoc.unesco.org/ark:/48223/pf0000074694. | UNData, http://data.un.org/Search.aspx?q=Latin+America. | WorldAtlas.com.

Fiestas Patrias parade float, East Chicago, 1926

Contributors

Authors

Nicole Martinez–LeGrand, a third-generation Hoosier Mexican American, has been examining Indiana's Mexican diaspora as the Indiana Historical Society's multicultural collections curator. In 2021 she won an outstanding community leadership award for her work, focusing on community building and development.

Daniel Gonzales earned a master's degree in museum studies from the University of Missouri–Saint Louis as an E. Desmond Lee Fellow. After working as a researcher, curator, and historian, he became director of exhibitions research at the Indiana Historical Society.

Sujey Vega is the faculty head for Arizona State University's American Studies program, as well as an associate professor of Women and Gender Studies and affiliate faculty member in the School of Transborder Studies and Religious Studies.

Index